Writing the Critical Essay

Euthanasia

An OPPOSING VIEWPOINTS® Guide

Lauri S. Friedman, *Book Editor*

OPPOSING
VIEWPOINTS®
SERIES

GREENHAVEN PRESS
A part of Gale, Cengage Learning

GALE
CENGAGE Learning

Detroit • New York • San Francisco • New Haven, Conn • Waterville, Maine • London

Christine Nasso, *Publisher*
Elizabeth Des Chenes, *Managing Editor*

© 2010 Greenhaven Press, a part of Gale, Cengage Learning

For more information, contact:
Greenhaven Press
27500 Drake Rd.
Farmington Hills, MI 48331-3535
Or you can visit our Internet site at gale.cengage.com

For product information and technology assistance, contact us at

Gale Customer Support, 1-800-877-4253
For permission to use material from this text or product, submit all requests online at
www.cengage.com/permissions

Further permissions questions can be e-mailed to permissionrequest@cengage.com

Articles in Greenhaven Press anthologies are often edited for length to meet page requirements. In addition, original titles of these works are changed to clearly present the main thesis and to explicitly indicate the author's opinion. Every effort is made to ensure that Greenhaven Press accurately reflects the original intent of the authors. Every effort has been made to trace the owners of copyrighted material.

Cover image © Frank Fife/AFP/Getty Images.

LIBRARY OF CONGRESS CATALOGING-IN-PUBLICATION DATA

Euthanasia / Lauri S. Friedman, book editor.
    p. cm. -- (Writing the critical essay: an opposing viewpoints guide)
Includes bibliographical references and index.
ISBN 978-0-7377-4562-7 (hardcover)
1. Euthanasia. I. Friedman, Lauri S.
R726.E7835 2009
179.7--dc22

                                                                    2009026392

Printed in the United States of America
1 2 3 4 5 6 7 13 12 11 10 09

CONTENTS

Examining the state of writing and how it is taught in the United States was the official purpose of the National Commission on Writing in America's Schools and Colleges. The commission, made up of teachers, school administrators, business leaders, and college and university presidents, released its first report in 2003. "Despite the best efforts of many educators," commissioners argued, "writing has not received the full attention it deserves." Among the findings of the commission was that most fourth-grade students spent less than three hours a week writing, that three-quarters of high school seniors never receive a writing assignment in their history or social studies classes, and that more than 50 percent of first-year students in college have problems writing error-free papers. The commission called for a "cultural sea change" that would increase the emphasis on writing for both elementary and secondary schools. These conclusions have made some educators realize that writing must be emphasized in the curriculum. As colleges are demanding an ever-higher level of writing proficiency from incoming students, schools must respond by making students more competent writers. In response to these concerns, the SAT, an influential standardized test used for college admissions, required an essay for the first time in 2005.

Books in the Writing the Critical Essay: An Opposing Viewpoints Guide series use the patented Opposing Viewpoints format to help students learn to organize ideas and arguments and to write essays using common critical writing techniques. Each book in the series focuses on a particular type of essay writing—including expository, persuasive, descriptive, and narrative—that students learn while being taught both the five-paragraph essay as well as longer pieces of writing that have an opinionated focus. These guides include everything necessary to help students research, outline, draft, edit, and ultimately write successful essays across the curriculum, including essays for the SAT.

Using Opposing Viewpoints

This series is inspired by and builds upon Greenhaven Press's acclaimed Opposing Viewpoints series. As in the parent series, each book in the Writing the Critical Essay series focuses on a timely and controversial social issue that provides lots of opportunities for creating thought-provoking essays. The first section of each volume begins with a brief introductory essay that provides context for the opposing viewpoints that follow. These articles are chosen for their accessibility and clearly stated views. The thesis of each article is made explicit in the article's title and is accentuated by Its pairing with an opposing or alternative view. These essays are both models of persuasive writing techniques and valuable research material that students can mine to write their own informed essays. Guided reading and discussion questions help lead students to key ideas and writing techniques presented in the selections.

The second section of each book begins with a preface discussing the format of the essays and examining characteristics of the featured essay type. Model five-paragraph and longer essays then demonstrate that essay type. The essays are annotated so that key writing elements and techniques are pointed out to the student. Sequential, step-by-step exercises help students construct and refine thesis statements; organize material into outlines; analyze and try out writing techniques; write transitions, introductions, and conclusions; and incorporate quotations and other researched material. Ultimately, students construct their own compositions using the designated essay type.

The third section of each volume provides additional research material and writing prompts to help the student. Additional facts about the topic of the book serve as a convenient source of supporting material for essays. Other features help students go beyond the book for their research. Like other Greenhaven Press books, each book in the Writing the Critical Essay series includes bibliographic listings of relevant periodical articles, books, Web sites, and organizations to contact.

Writing the Critical Essay: An Opposing Viewpoints Guide will help students master essay techniques that can be used in any discipline.

Do Americans Have the "Right to Die"?

Whether Americans have a right to die is at the heart of the passionate arguments made both for and against euthanasia. Legally, the battle to articulate and achieve a right to die has been met with many obstacles and challenges. The first was in 1952, when the Euthanasia Society of America petitioned the United Nations Human Rights Commission to declare that people dying from an incurable disease have the right to die. The United Nations did not grant the request, believing that its efforts to promote human rights were best applied to matters regarding life, not death. Furthermore, the UN's Universal Declaration of Human Rights (UNDHR)—one of the most widely respected and cited human rights documents—had been adopted just four years earlier, as a response to the atrocities committed during World War II. It outlined more than thirty human rights that are focused on improving a person's experience in *life* by ensuring them greater access to education, food, water, work, health care, happiness, property, and so on. The commission no doubt worried that any endorsement of death was counterproductive to its mission of improving life.

The Supreme Court agreed with this logic many years later, when in 1997 it heard arguments in the related cases *Washington v. Glucksberg* and *Vacco v. Quill*. It was determined through these cases that Americans do not in fact have a constitutional right to die. Believing, like many Americans and the United Nations, that life is a precious, valuable thing, the Supreme Court felt it was neither appropriate nor useful to protect a person's right to end it. Moreover, the judges reflected a popular sentiment that society should not focus on achieving rights to die until a person's rights in life have been thoroughly

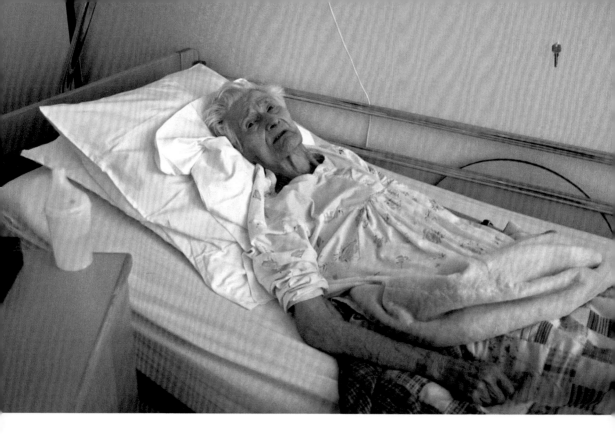

The right to die is a highly controversial issue with no easy solution.

guaranteed. As scholar Rhoda Olkin expresses it, "There is an existential absurdity to developing laws and guidelines on the right to die when citizens do not have the right to live."[1] Olkin and others urge people to put more time and energy into outlining policies that will make human life more bearable and reduce the desire and need to champion unnatural death.

But supporters of euthanasia see the issue as one of personal freedom, in line with the right to freely control any other aspect of their life. They cite the right to a dignified, merciful death as being part and parcel of each American's constitutional right to life, liberty, and pursuit of happiness—in this case, the pursuit of happiness is the pursuit of relief from pain and suffering. If a terminally ill, suffering person judges that death is preferable to life, euthanasia supporters say the state should not stand in the way of letting them end theirs, any more than it should prevent a person from making any other big decision that influences the outcome of their life.

Patients have sought this right in places where euthanasia is illegal, such as France. In that country, Chantal Sebire, who in 2002 was diagnosed with a rare, severely deforming type of nose cancer, sparked a national controversy when she petitioned the government to let her receive euthanasia. In addition to being in excruciating pain, Sebire had also lost her senses of smell, taste, and sight. Said Sebire, "One would not allow an animal to go through what I have endured."[2] However, despite overwhelming support for the woman's plight, the court rejected her appeal. Shortly afterward, Sebire committed suicide privately, which caused her supporters to complain that she had to unfairly cross into death in what was likely a more painful, scary experience than a regulated euthanasia would have been. Even more than pity for Sebire, the court's rejection of her request was criticized by her supporters as a classic case of state "paternalism"—or when the government thinks it knows what is best for people. They said that denying a sick, suffering person the right to end their life is a denial of the fact that their life is theirs to begin with.

But not everyone believes that denying people the right to die compromises their freedom in any real way. As euthanasia opponents point out, people accept government interference on their behalf in plenty of matters. Americans commonly accept—and even widely support—laws that tell them where they can smoke, what medications they need a prescription for, and even when they are allowed to water their lawn or wash their car (increasingly common measures in drought-stricken areas). Most Americans do not regard these laws as being paternalistic or overbearing—they accept them as the result of government doing its job of guarding public health and safety. So, too, say euthanasia opponents, is state opposition to euthanasia.

Finally, opponents warn it is a mistake to frame euthanasia as a matter of choice or liberty because it denies the biggest problem with the issue: that not everyone who might be euthanized is acting freely or rationally. In other words, it is feared that people in a coma or other noncommunicative state might be euthanized without their permission; or, those who give permission might be acting out of a pressure to relieve their family members of the financial burden of their care. As evangelical leader Albert Mohler coldly puts it, "Once a society adopts a *right* to die as a matter of policy, a *duty* to die cannot be far behind."[3] Many Americans worry that making euthanasia more commonplace will encourage people to choose death too hastily or for the wrong reasons.

Whether Americans should or do have a right to die is one of the many issues explored in *Writing the Critical Essay: Euthanasia*. The morality of euthanasia, its related risks, and to what extent it threatens vulnerable groups of people are explored in passionately argued viewpoints

A person's first experience with euthanasia is usually the difficult decision to euthanize a beloved family pet.

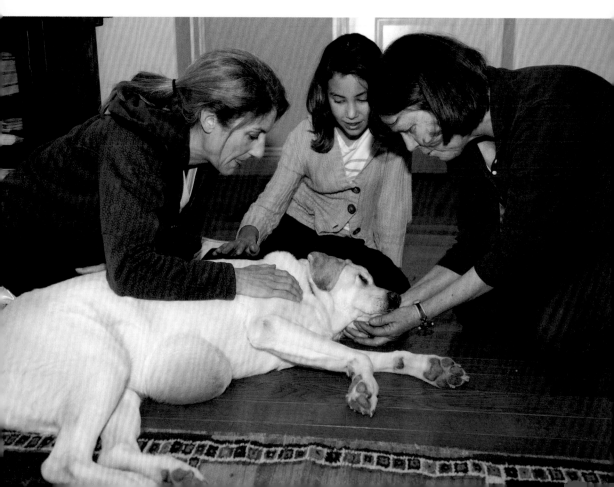

and model essays. Thought-provoking writing exercises and step-by-step instructions help readers write their own five-paragraph persuasive essays on this compelling and personal subject.

Notes

1. Rhoda Olkin, "Why I Changed My Mind About Physician-Assisted Suicide," *Journal of Disability Policy Studies*, vol. 16, no. 1, Summer 2005, p. 69.
2. British Broadcasting Company, "France Rejects Right-to-Die Plea," March 17, 2008. http://news.bbc.co.uk/2/hi/health/7301566.stm.
3. Albert Mohler, "A Threat to the Disabled . . . and to Us All," AlbertMohler.com, August 9, 2007. www.albertmohler.com/blog_print.php?id = 983.

Section One: Opposing Viewpoints on Euthanasia

Euthanasia Is Murder

John Burns

John Burns is a doctor in Citrus Heights, California. In the following essay he argues that euthanasia amounts to murder. Burns says that causing the unnatural death of a sick person robs them of the chance to get better on their own. He discusses a case from Hurricane Katrina in which, under dire circumstances, medical staff euthanized four patients at a New Orleans hospital. Because the city was flooded and had no access to electricity or supplies, the doctors and nurses thought it would be more humane to euthanize the patients than to let them die slowly over the course of the disaster. Burns says they had no right to make this choice, and he has every reason to expect that the patients could have lived through the disaster. He concludes that euthanasia is a form of murder that should never be accepted or encouraged.

Consider the following questions:

1. Who are Anna Pou, Lori Budo, and Cheri Landry?
2. Who is Angela McManus, and what happened to her mother during Hurricane Katrina?
3. According to Burns, what should doctors never become "dispensers" of?

Butch was a one-year-old Rottweiler-boxer mix—he looked like a pit bull on steroids. I came home one day to find him very sick, apparently poisoned. Taking him to a veterinarian, I got the bad news: "He's real sick and he's not going to make it." I asked the doc if there wasn't something that could be done but he assured me it was hopeless. "He's dying and he's suffering a lot. We should put him down." I have to admit that the additional $90 fee for "putting Butch to sleep" probably played into my decision, but mostly I held on to a slim hope that he might make it, so I told the vet I was bringing Butch home. He strongly disagreed. As you've probably guessed, we nursed him for a couple of weeks and eventually he got back to his big healthy self. It was my first experience with the veterinary ethic—relieving suffering through "euthanasia," or as it roughly translates, "good death."

Fine for Animals but Not Humans

While it may make sense with animals, the specter of physicians accepting the veterinary ethic of dispensing death to end suffering ought to scare the "heck" out of us. Apparently that's what happened in the aftermath of Hurricane Katrina[1] when a physician and two nurses decided to play God and end the lives of a number of their patients with a deadly cocktail of morphine and Versed, a sedative. On July 18, [2006,] Anna Pou, M.D., and nurses Lori Budo and Cheri Landry were arrested on the charge of being "a principal to second degree murder." The three are charged in the deaths of four persons, aged 61, 67, 90, and 97, who were patients at the New Orleans Memorial Medical Center. Louisiana Attorney General Charles C. Foti suggested that there might be more victims to be identified. As for the four victims Foti said, "This is not euthanasia. This is homicide. These patients would have lived through an evacuation if they had not been killed."

The Slippery Slope of Euthanasia

Advocates for euthanasia routinely chide opponents that "slippery slope" arguments are fallacious and irrelevant. A decision to allow euthanasia in some cases, they say, does not in fact open the door for the killing of yet others. Tragically, however, the "slippery slope" argument is neither fallacious nor irrelevant, as recent developments in the Netherlands have made graphically clear. Once doctors are allowed to choose death over life, the resulting Culture of Death will inevitably discount human life in other contexts as well.

Albert Mohler, "Euthanasia for Newborns—Killing in the Netherlands," AlbertMohler.com, March 14, 2005. www.albertmohler.com/commentary_read.php?cdate = 2005-03-14.

---

1. The 2005 hurricane that flooded New Orleans and left more than eighteen hundred people dead.

A Lethal Decision

Three days after Katrina, the Memorial Medical Center was flooded on the first floor and was without electricity. The temperatures hit 100 degrees and the situation was unquestionably a difficult one. Most patients and staff were evacuated by boat or helicopter; however, transporting some patients proved quite difficult, especially those who were very ill.

According to the affidavit filed by Foti, witnesses testified that Susan Mulderick, the "Incident Commander" at Memorial, told them, "We're not leaving any living patients behind." Other witnesses testified that the two nurses and Dr. Pou told them a decision had been made to "administer lethal doses." Dr. Pou, who was apparently unfamiliar with the patients, assumed they were all unconscious. When a staffer informed her that the 61-year-old man, although paralyzed, was "conscious, awake and alert," Dr. Pou ordered that he be sedated. When the staffer refused, Dr. Pou allegedly said she was going to tell the patient she was giving him something to help with dizziness. Witnesses testified that Dr. Pou entered the room with a syringe and closed the door. Post-mortem tissue samples taken from the patient showed lethal doses of morphine and Versed. Neither drug had been prescribed for him previously.

Mug shots show (left to right) Dr. Anna Pou and nurses Cheri Landry and Lori Budo after they were arrested on charges of giving lethal injections to four patients in a New Orleans hospital during Hurricane Katrina.

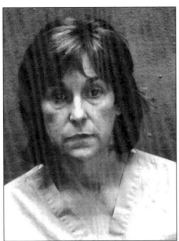

Not Mercy but Murder

Apparently not wanting witnesses to their "acts of mercy," those involved ordered everyone removed from the medical center. Angela McManus had been staying with her mother who was recovering from a blood infection. When she refused to leave, she was forced out by armed police officers who reportedly had their guns drawn. According to Ms. McManus, her mother was doing well when she

Different Forms of Euthanasia

The term *euthanasia* comes from a Greek word that literally means "dying well" or "a good death." Euthanasia is an umbrella term that is often used to refer to several distinct practices:

Term	Practice	Historical Example
Passive euthanasia	When a patient's death is caused by the removal of life support or by withholding life-saving treatments.	What happened in the case of Terri Schiavo, who died in 2005 after she was disconnected from life support. Schiavo had been in a persistent vegetative state for fifteen years.
Voluntary or active euthanasia	When a patient asks a doctor to directly cause their death by injecting them with a lethal substance.	What Dr. Jack Kevorkian did to patients such as Thomas Youk. Youk was suffering from a terminal illness when he asked Kevorkian to cause his death.
Physician-assisted suicide	When a doctor prescribes a lethal medication to a patient. The patient then uses it to cause their own death.	What more than 340 people since 1997 have done under Oregon's Death with Dignity Act. Their doctors prescribed them lethal medication, which they self-administered in their own homes at the time of their choosing.

Compiled by editor.

left, but mysteriously died later that day, although she is not among the four victims named in the affidavit. McManus said, "I need some answers. Euthanasia is something you do to a horse or an animal. When you do it to people it's called murder."

Unfortunately, many in the medical community don't agree with Ms. McManus. Dr. Daniel Nuss, Dr. Pou's boss at the Louisiana State University Health Sciences Center, said, "This is vilifying the heroes. I think it's presumptuous for the attorney general or anyone else to try to assign blame for what happened under such desperate circumstances." A perusal of medical discussion boards on the Internet reveals a split in the opinions from physicians regarding this case, but the majority seems to be supporting Dr. Pou.

Angela McManus, whose mother mysteriously died in chaotic conditions at a New Orleans hospital during Hurricane Katrina.

A Doctor's Job Is to Save, Not Kill

Dr. Pou said: "There were patients there that had orders of do not resuscitate, in other words if they died, to allow them to die naturally and not use any heroic methods to resuscitate them. We did everything within our power to give the best treatment that we could to the patients in the hospital, to make them comfortable." Pou is a very educated physician and surgeon. If she is unable to distinguish between "allowing them to die naturally" and giving them a shot that kills them, we're all in trouble.

Perhaps you should ask your physician where he or she stands on this issue. Does your doctor stand by the dictum credited to [ancient Greek physician] Hippocrates, "First, do no harm"? Does your doctor take a stand against physicians becoming dispensers of death? If not, maybe it's time to find a new doctor.

Analyze the essay:

1. John Burns opens his essay by telling the story of his dog Butch. What is the story, and how does it relate to the rest of the essay? Why do you think he chose to open his essay with this anecdote?

2. Both Burns, the author of this essay, and Paul Heslin, the author of the following essay, are doctors. Yet Burns believes euthanasia is murder, while Heslin believes euthanasia is merciful. Does it surprise you that two doctors think differently on this issue? With which doctor do you ultimately agree?

Euthanasia Is Not Murder

Paul Heslin

In the following essay Paul Heslin argues that euthanasia is humane and compassionate when applied to the right situations. He says that people who would be euthanized are going to die anyway, and euthanasia saves them from suffering terrible pain. He argues that people who worry that legalizing euthanasia would lead to mass murder are wrong—euthanasia does not lead to the widespread killing of animals, and thus there is no reason for people to think it will lead to the widespread killing of humans. Heslin says that we euthanize our pets to save them from agony and suffering, and in his opinion, we should extend this same compassion to humans. He concludes that euthanasia is not an act of murder but one of sympathy and even love.

Paul Heslin is a medical doctor, a personal and business coach, and a family therapist.

Consider the following questions:

1. According to Heslin, what is the "floodgates theory"? Why does he think it is not helpful in making decisions about euthanasia?
2. What are some of the words that Heslin says are used to describe the death of animals vs. the death of humans?
3. Who is Sandy? How does she fit into the author's argument?

Putting the dog down is a common euphemism. Is it kindness or murder? We love our pets. We like our patients. We put our pets down. We keep our patients

Paul Heslin, "Language Hides the Realities of Death," *Irish Medical Times,* August 2008. © Reed Business Information 2007. Reproduced by permission.

The author believes we euthanize our pets to save them pain and suffering, and we should show the same compassion toward humans.

alive. We put our pets down when we want to save them suffering. We keep our patients alive despite our occasional failure to keep severe pain at bay and their calls for peace.

A Common Story

[The soap opera] *Fair City* dealt with euthanasia on a recent Sunday evening. The following Monday lunchtime brought a call to Jo Duffy [a radio DJ who hosts a show called *Liveline*]. The caller said that many years ago, she injected her dying dad with anaesthetic that she got because she worked in the industry. She sounded very compassionate and her dad sounded very much in pain and now very dead. I did not know what to think. She said that it was done out of care and that she would do it again.

It was one of those moments when the interviewer asks some great questions, but you feel that the most obvious one is avoided. It was clamouring in my head. Ask this question: "Lady, why are you telling the Irish nation, through *Liveline*, that you committed a crime? Surely you know that the police will have to follow this up. What are you doing? Are you mad? What is your story? Why? Why? Why now?" More interesting, even, to me was the comparison made between our treatment of pets and our treatment of humans.

"We treat our dogs with more care than our dying." "My mother begged me to help her die after six months of unbearable pain." "I wouldn't want to go through what my mum went through." "It is real cruelty that we let people die in pain when they want to go." "They treat animals better than they treat humans."

Irrational Fear

We have a fear of the floodgates with humans. If we allowed any form of euthanasia, then the floodgates would be open and anyone could 'kill' those that were no longer considered useful. We have no fear that owners or vets killing their pets or horses, when this is the practical thing to do, will lead to widespread killing of pets. There's no fear of floodgates when it comes to animals.

The floodgates theory is often used in human logic to stymie any change or new solutions to difficult and complex human dilemmas of care. It helps keep the status quo even as the rest of the world changes around this same status quo. Even as patients feel robbed of their right to depart this life at a time of their choosing. Even as they feel they are treated most cruelly by society at this time, their time of most need.

Euthanasia Is the Compassionate Choice

As a nation, we seem to care more for the survival of those who are incurable, in enormous pain, and want to end their lives peacefully, than we do for our young men and women sent off to war. We are concerned with the humanity of survival. We have protections against anthrax and polio. We wear seat belts. The Food and Drug Administration guarantees the safety of what we eat and the medications we imbibe. Why not show the same humanness towards those who suffer near the end of their lives?

Jerome Greenblatt, "The Case for Euthanasia," *Let Life In*, April 2, 2008. www.letlifein.com/2008/04/02/to-die-or-not-to-die.

Euthanasia Is Compassionate
for Animals *and* Humans

Dedicating your life to allaying human suffering and working for other humans and then discovering that 'they' won't allow you to pass peacefully on your final journey is a bitter irony. 'What if?' can sound so distant and so callous when you are tortured. We use different language for animals. This is hardly surprising, given our conviction of our superiority, difference and special status in the animal kingdom. We put animals 'to sleep'. We 'murder' humans—even when it is with the compassion and pragmatism of an honest vet. I am not aware of any equivalent word for 'euthanasia' for animals.

It Is Easier to Blame than Grieve

Having said all that, I still clearly remember over 35 years ago, when my beloved pet dog Sandy, a golden cocker spaniel, was put down by our local vet in Portlaoise. I blamed him for many years. I think I even blamed the vet for the disease and old age that caused my dog's demise. The vet was guilty by association. He was there and was therefore responsible. It was easier to blame the unknown distant vet, rather than my parents who must have been involved in this action, or God who must have had even more to say about these life-and-death decisions.

Looking back now, I recognise that we humans do make some odd decisions. We are all emotionally irrational sometimes. The vet was doing the practical and caring thing and giving peace to my Sandy, whose future was doomed with pain and indignity. Veterinary is indeed a noble, caring and pragmatic profession.

We All Deserve Compassion

I remember a discussion about euthanasia being discussed on RTE [Ireland's national television and radio broadcaster] many years ago. A man said he would like five people to decide his end. These included himself, his

Euthanasia Around the World

Various forms of euthanasia are legal in four countries.

	Belgium	Netherlands	United States (Oregon & Washington)	Switzerland
What is legal?				
Euthanasia	Yes	Yes	No	No
Physician-assisted suicide	No	Yes	Yes	Yes
Restricting preconditions				
The patient must have a terminal illness?	No	No	Yes	No
Is a second medical opinion mandatory?	Yes	Yes	Yes	No
The patient has made repeated requests over a period of time?	Yes	Yes	Yes	No
How many patients?	About 0.6% of all deaths.	1.5% of all deaths; however, this does not include the large number of cases that go unreported.	Less than 0.1% of all Oregon deaths.	About 0.2% of all Swiss deaths.
The role of the pharmacist				
Is any mention of the role of the pharmacist included in the relevant legislation?	Yes	No	Yes	No
Do pharmacists have professional guidance?	Yes	Yes	Yes (but limited to guiding principles)	No

The author, a physician, believes that a doctor's job is to alleviate suffering, and sometime that includes hastening death.

best friend, the vet, his spiritual advisor and a doctor. He chose the vet for a pragmatic approach to quality-of-life issues.

There seems to be a diversity of passionate views about dealing caringly with end of life (death) issues. Many seem to feel that one black and white answer will solve a complex variety of situations. However, we live in a diverse culture now. Some who don't believe in euthanasia expect that they have the right to impose their views on those who do believe in euthanasia. Is there not room for both views?

I, for one, want a vet at my war table. I don't do meaningless pain very well. I expect that right to self-determination. Let me pass peacefully when my time comes.

Analyze the essay:

1. Paul Heslin relates a story about a man who says he would like five specific people to decide his death—himself, his best friend, his veterinarian, his spiritual adviser, and his doctor. Why does he say the man wanted to include his veterinarian? Do you agree or disagree with this choice?

2. Both Heslin and Burns (the author of the previous essay) used animals to make their arguments about euthanasia. After reading both essays, do you think the same standards should be applied to end-of-life matters for animals as to end-of-life matters for humans? Should different standards be applied? Why or why not?

Euthanasia Is Merciful

Peter Singer

Peter Singer is a professor of bioethics at Princeton University. In the following essay he examines a practice in the Netherlands called the Groningen Protocol, which allows doctors to end the lives of severely disabled infants. Singer explains the infants are typically born with a debilitating disease that would not allow them to live any semblance of a normal life. They may have brain damage, or parts of their spine may not have fully formed. They may be completely reliant on respirators, or may require twenty-four-hour care for the rest of their life. Such infants are expected to live lives of such pain and suffering that Singer says death is a more merciful option for them. In these cases Singer supports the decision of Dutch doctors to, with the permission of parents, end the lives of such infants. He concludes it is the mark of a humane society that prevents terrible suffering and focuses its resources on caring for those who have a better chance at living life.

Consider the following questions:

1. Who are Eduard Verhagen and Pieter Sauer?
2. Why does Singer say that pro-life groups in the United States should not criticize what is done in the Netherlands?
3. What does Singer say is the infant mortality rate in the United States? How does this compare with the infant mortality rate in the Netherlands?

Peter Singer, "Pulling Back the Curtain on the Mercy Killing of Newborns," *Los Angeles Times*, March 11, 2005. Copyright © 2008 *Los Angeles Times*. Reproduced by permission of the author.

In [the March 10, 2005] *New England Journal of Medicine*, two doctors from the University Medical Center Groningen in the Netherlands outline the circumstances in which doctors in their hospital have, in 22 cases over seven years, carried out euthanasia on newborn infants. All of these cases were reported to a district attorney's office in the Netherlands. None of the doctors were prosecuted.

Eduard Verhagen and Pieter Sauer divide into three groups the newborns for whom decisions about ending life might be made.

Three Categories for Euthanasia
The first consists of infants who would die soon after birth even if all existing medical resources were employed to prolong their lives.

Dutch ministers and legislators defend the Netherlands euthanasia laws and urge Parliament to give final approval to the law in 2001.

American Opinions on End-of-Life Issues

End-of-life issues are complicated and personal. In 2007 a poll conducted jointly by the Associated Press and Ipsos found the following attitudes and opinions on a variety of end-of-life issues.

"Which comes closest to your view? In all circumstances, doctors and nurses should do everything possible to save the life of a patient. Sometimes there are circumstances where a patient should be allowed to die."

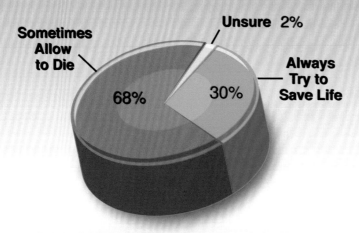

Unsure 2%

Sometimes Allow to Die

68%

30%

Always Try to Save Life

"Do you think it should be legal or illegal for doctors to help terminally ill patients end their own life by giving them a prescription for fatal drugs?"

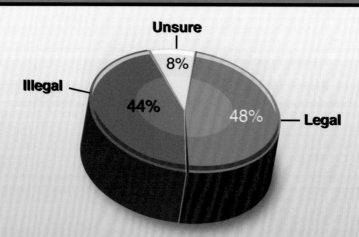

Unsure

8%

Illegal

44%

48% — Legal

"If you were seriously ill with a terminal disease, would you consider ending your own life, or not?"

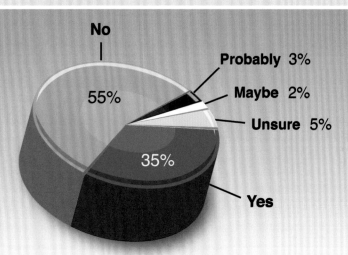

No
55%

Probably 3%

Maybe 2%

Unsure 5%

35%

Yes

"Do you think that Michigan doctor Jack Kevorkian should have been jailed for assisting terminally ill people to end their own life, or not?"

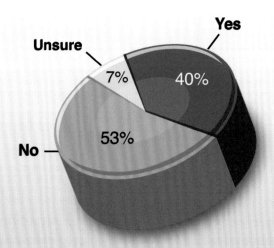

Unsure

Yes

7%

40%

53%

No

Taken from: Associated Press–Ipsos, May 22–24, 2007.

In the second group are infants who require intensive care, such as a respirator, to keep them alive, and for whom the expectations regarding their future are "very grim." These are infants with severe brain damage. If they can survive beyond intensive care, they will still have a very poor quality of life.

The third group includes infants with a "hopeless prognosis" and who also are victims of "unbearable suffering." For example, in the third group was "a child with the most serious form of spina bifida," the failure of the spinal cord to form and close properly. Yet infants in group three may no longer be dependent on intensive care.

Letting Severely Sick Infants Die

It is this third group that creates the controversy because their lives cannot be ended simply by withdrawing intensive care. Instead, at the University Medical Center Groningen, if suffering cannot be relieved and no improvement can be expected, the physicians will discuss with the parents whether this is a case in which death "would be more humane than continued life." If the parents agree that this is the case, and the team of physicians also agrees—as well as an independent physician not otherwise associated with the patient—the infant's life may be ended.

American "pro-life" groups will no doubt say that this is just another example of the slippery slope that the Netherlands began to slide down once it permitted voluntary euthanasia 20 years ago. But before they begin denouncing the Groningen doctors, they should take a look at what is happening in the United States.

Give Me the Mercy of Euthanasia

I no longer accept this enduring pain, and this protruding eye that nothing can be done about. . . . I want to go out celebrating, surrounded by my children, friends, and doctors before I'm put to sleep definitively at dawn.

Chantal Sebire, quoted in Bruce Crumley, "Making a Case for Euthanasia," *Time*, March 15, 2008. www.time.com/time/world/article/0,8599,172 2728,00.html.

It Is Moral to Relieve Suffering

One thing is undisputed: Infants with severe problems are allowed to die in the U.S. These are infants in the first two of the three groups identified by Verhagen and Sauer. Some of them—those in the second group—can live for many years if intensive care is continued. Nevertheless, U.S. doctors, usually in consultation with parents, make decisions to withdraw intensive care. This happens openly, in Catholic as well as non-Catholic hospitals.

I have taken my Princeton students to St. Peter's University Hospital, a Catholic facility in New Brunswick, N.J., that has a major neonatal intensive care unit, where Dr. Mark Hiatt, the unit director, has described cases in which he has withdrawn intensive care from infants with severe brain damage.

Tens of thousands of protesters gathered outside the Hague, in the Netherlands, in April 2001 to protest the government's decision to pass euthanasia laws.

Among neonatologists in the U.S. and the Netherlands, there is widespread agreement that sometimes it is ethically acceptable to end the life of a newborn infant with severe medical problems. Even the Roman Catholic Church accepts that it is not always required to use "extraordinary" means of life support and that a respirator can be considered "extraordinary."

Sometimes It Is Acceptable to End Life

The only serious dispute is whether it is acceptable to end the life of infants in Verhagen and Sauer's third group, that is, infants who are no longer dependent on intensive care for survival. To put this another way: The dispute is no longer about whether it is justifiable to end an infant's life if it won't be worth living but whether that end may be brought about by active means, or only by the withdrawal of treatment.

I believe the Groningen protocol to be based on the sound ethical perception that the means by which death occurs is less significant, ethically, than the decision that it is better that an infant's life should end. If it is sometimes acceptable to end the lives of infants in group two—and virtually no one denies this—then it is also sometimes acceptable to end the lives of infants in group three.

And, on the basis of comments made to me by some physicians, I am sure that the lives of infants in group three are sometimes ended in the U.S. But this is never reported or publicly discussed, for fear of prosecution. That means that standards governing when such actions are justified cannot be appropriately debated, let alone agreed upon.

A Sound Health-Care System

In the Netherlands, on the other hand, as Verhagen and Sauer write, "obligatory reporting with the aid of a protocol and subsequent assessment of euthanasia in newborns help us to clarify the decision-making process." There are many who will think that the existence of 22 cases of infant euthanasia over seven years at one hospital in the Netherlands shows that it is a society that has less respect for human life than the United States. But I'd suggest that they take a look at the difference in infant mortality rates between the two countries.

The CIA World Factbook shows that the U.S. has an infant mortality rate of 6.63 per 1,000 live births, the Netherlands 5.11. If the U.S. had infant mortality rates as low as the Netherlands, there would be 6,296 fewer infant deaths nationwide each year.

Building a healthcare system in the U.S. as good as that in the Netherlands—as measured by infant mortality—is far more worthy of the attention of those who value human life than the deaths of 22 tragically afflicted infants.

Analyze the essay:

1. In this essay Peter Singer uses history, facts, and examples to make his argument that euthanasia is merciful. However, he only uses one quotation to support his point. If you were to rewrite this article and insert more quotations, what authorities might you quote from? Where would you place these quotations to bolster the points Singer makes?

2. To make his argument, Singer focuses on the case of severely disabled infants. If you had a baby that was so disabled it required medical machinery or around-the-clock care to live, what decision would you make? Would you feel it is more merciful to keep the infant alive, or more merciful to end its life? In your answer, explain what factors would influence your decision.

Euthanasia Is Not Merciful

Paul K. Longmore

In the following essay Paul K. Longmore argues that euthanasia is never merciful. He tells the story of David Rivlin, a thirty-eight-year-old quadriplegic who was eventually allowed by the state of Michigan to die. Longmore explains that Americans thought it was natural that Rivlin would want to die—he was unable to walk, breathe on his own, use the bathroom by himself, or have a relationship or a career. As a result, many people thought that letting Rivlin die would be an act of mercy. But Longmore says that Rivlin was prevented from doing those things not because of his disability but because of the limitations society puts on disabled people. Longmore points out that no one helped Rivlin overcome his disability. The people and institutions charged with his care made him feel like a burden, and so he became one. Longmore concludes it is wrong to assume that some lives are not worth living. He says the people who encouraged Rivlin's death were not being merciful, but selfish and discriminatory.

Longmore is a professor of history and director of the Institute on Disability at San Francisco State University. He is disabled and relies on a ventilator to breathe.

Consider the following questions:
1. How does the author say David Rivlin became a quadriplegic?
2. What questions does Longmore say the media should have asked Rivlin when his relationship with Zoe Dixon ended?
3. According to Longmore, what blocked Rivlin's efforts to live the life he wanted?

Paul K. Longmore, "Policy, Prejudice, and Reality: Two Cases of Physician-Assisted Suicide," *Journal of Disability Studies*, vol. 16, Summer 2005, pp. 38–45. Copyright © 2005 PRO-ED. Reprinted by permission of Sage Publications.

"Tiring of Life Without Freedom," ran the *People* magazine headline, "Quadriplegic David Rivlin Chooses to Die Among Friends." The story that followed told how for three years David Rivlin had lain in the same bed at the Oak Hill Care Center outside Detroit, his eyes wandering over the same limited landscape: white ceiling tiles, turquoise walls and drab beige curtains framing a view of a brick wall. He listened to the radio, and when his bed was raised he was able to watch TV or a movie cassette, but nothing could tune out the sound that symbolized his ultimate imprisonment: the incessant whir of a respirator sitting on a chipped wooden nightstand close enough to allow its hose to reach through the hole in his throat. . . . For the 38-year-old Rivlin, it was only a cruel semblance of life. Since he broke his neck in a swimming accident at age 20, paralysis had slowly crept up his spine, rendering him a quadriplegic and unable to breathe on his own.

Quadriplegic David Rivlin waits in his hospital room while the Michigan state legislature debates his petition for the right to die.

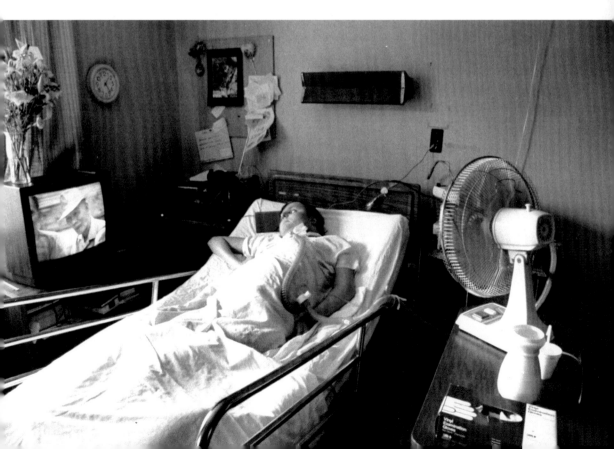

A Timeline of Euthanasia and Physician-Assisted Suicide

4th Century B.C.: The Hippocratic oath is developed in ancient Greece. Among other things, it instructs healers to "do no harm."

1828: The first American law to outlaw assisted suicide is passed in New York on December 10.

1950: The World Medical Association officially condemns the practice of euthanasia.

1961: Although suicide is decriminalized in Great Britain, a maximum penalty for assisting a suicide is established at fourteen years.

1972: The first national hearings are held by the U.S. Senate Special Commission on Aging to discuss dying with dignity and assisted suicide.

1974: The first American hospice opens in New Haven, Connecticut.

1988: The Unitarian Universalist Association of Congregations becomes the first religious organization to pass a resolution that allows the terminally ill to be aided in dying.

1990: Physician Jack Kevorkian helps Janet Adkins to commit suicide in Michigan. Adkins's death is the first of 130 suicides in which Kevorkian will assist.

1994: The Oregon Death with Dignity Act is passed, making Oregon the first U.S. state to legalize physician-assisted suicide. However, a judge prevents it from going into effect.

1996: Australia's Northern Territory legalizes voluntary euthanasia. A year later, however, the federal government vetoes the law after four terminally ill patients take their own lives.

1997: In the cases *Washington v. Glucksberg* and *Vacco v. Quill* the Supreme Court rules that Americans do not have a constitutional right to die.

- President Bill Clinton signs the Assisted Suicide Funding Restriction Act of 1997. This makes it illegal to use federal funds to cause a patient's death.

- Physician-assisted suicide becomes able to be used in Oregon after residents vote 60 to 40 percent in favor of retaining the Death with Dignity Act.

1998: *60 Minutes* airs a video of Kevorkian administering a lethal injection to Thomas Youk, a terminally ill patient.

1999: A Michigan court convicts Kevorkian of Youk's murder and sentences him to ten to twenty years in prison.

2002: Euthanasia becomes legal in the Netherlands in April. The next month, Belgium decriminalizes euthanasia.

2003: Attorney General John Ashcroft tries to have Oregon's Death with Dignity Act overturned on the grounds that it does not serve a legitimate medical purpose.

2005: Although Switzerland has allowed assisted suicide since the 1940s, in December 2005 a hospital allows the procedure to take place there rather than at a private residence.

2006: The Supreme Court, in a 6–3 opinion in *Gonzales v. Oregon*, upholds Oregon's Death with Dignity Act.

2007: After serving eight years, Jack Kevorkian is released from prison on June 1.

2008: Washington becomes the second U.S. state to legalize physician-assisted suicide.

Compiled by editor.

A Man Who Thought Death Was Better

In May 1989, David Rivlin petitioned the Oakland County Circuit Court for permission to have a doctor assist him to die. He wanted the doctor to sedate him and then disconnect his ventilator. In July 1989, Judge Hilda Crane ruled that his assisted death would be nothing more than a refusal of medical treatment . . .

The court ruling, the support of Rivlin's "choice" by both right-to-die activists and some medical practitioners, and media accounts of this case all misstated the basic issue. *People* summed up the common public reaction when it described Rivlin's disability as "his ultimate imprisonment" and said that it reduced him to "a cruel semblance of life". It was not David Rivlin's respirator that "imprisoned" him in that bleak nursing home for three horrible years. It was not his disability that reduced him to "a cruel semblance of life." Rivlin's freedom, and finally his life, were taken by a system that segregated him, refused him the right of self-determination (except to die), and allowed him to be exploited for the profit of the nursing home industry. Nonetheless, the dominant viewpoint consistently made his disability the cause of his confinement in that bleak nursing home. That perspective misread much of what Rivlin himself said about the grueling experience that finally made his life unendurable.

Society Confused Mercy with Pity

David Rivlin said, "I wanted a wife, children, to be able to do lots of things". At a nursing home in Dearborn, Michigan, he and a nondisabled office worker, Zoe Dixon, fell in love. They got engaged. In 1980, he moved into her home. According to Rivlin, "it lasted about a year. The burden of my being a quadriplegic broke us up".

None of the reporters who covered the story asked what Rivlin meant when he called himself a "burden." Neither they nor any of the nondisabled people around him had enough knowledge about the experience of people with significant physical disabilities to pose the important questions about his and Dixon's relationship. Did she provide the personal assistance he needed? Was she the only one to provide him with this aid, or was she able to get some respite? Did he have to depend only on her, or was he able to employ paid workers so that he, too, could get some relief from exclusive reliance on her? Was she paid by the state as his chore worker? Did they know about government marriage "disincentives"? Were they aware that if they married, David would lose any financial aid the state might give him to hire chore providers? How did those policies affect their relationship and plans? Did they keep their relationship secret from the state and county? If David had gotten an amount adequate to hire such workers, and if those benefits would have continued after he married Zoe, and if he could have relied on someone other than Zoe to meet his physical needs, would their relationship have had a chance? No one asked any of these questions. None of the reporters, nor the attorney who petitioned the court for Rivlin's right to doctor-assisted death, nor the physician who facilitated his suicide, nor anyone close to him in his final days had enough knowledge about David Rivlin or physically disabled people to raise any of these questions.

> ## There Is No Such Thing as a "Right to Die"
>
> To ask if euthanasia should be legalized is not merely to ask whether an in-principle "right to die" exists in moral terms. Proponents of euthanasia are also asking the state to take part, through its laws and its representatives, in the actual act of terminating life. In order to protect all of us, I believe that the state must say that whilst there is a right to life, there is no right to death. People die. But the state shouldn't kill them.
>
> Alex Deane, "The Case Against Euthanasia," ConservativeHome, May 16, 2006. http://conservativehome.blogs.com/platform/2006/05/alex_deane_the_.html.

A Disabled Life Is Very Worth Living

In addition to marriage and family, David Rivlin dreamed of a professional career. In college, he majored in philosophy and wanted, according to varying accounts, either to teach philosophy or to become a psychotherapist. One reporter assumed that "his dreams disappeared as he was pounded and torn by the churning surf" in his 1971

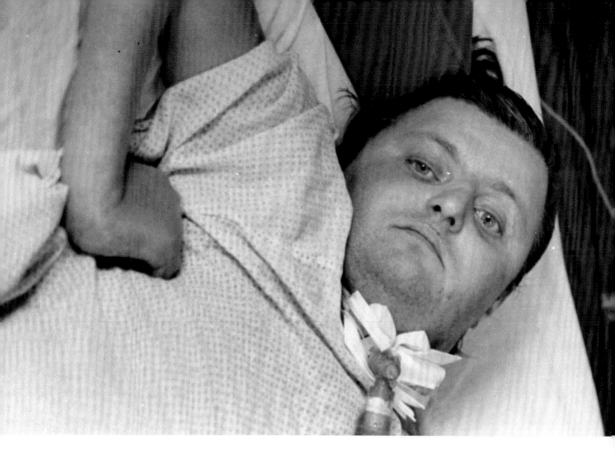

David Rivlin is shown shortly before his death. The author argues that his death was not an act of mercy.

accident. That journalistic rhetoric, designed to tug at readers' heartstrings, is inaccurate. The fact is that from 1974 to 1979, Rivlin continued to pursue his education. Returning from California to Michigan, he enrolled in Oakland University and studied philosophy. Neither his spinal cord injury nor his later use of a ventilator need have destroyed his dreams. The author of the article you are reading is a university professor who uses a ventilator in the classroom. . . .

At first in the nursing home, David Rivlin clung to the hope that he might escape. At last, his imprisonment made him despondent and despairing. He had few visitors. "In the last two years I never once found him reading or listening to music or talking to someone," recounted a friend. "He just lay there, looking straight up at the ceiling or dozing".

According to one account, "he's weary of being a burden on others and . . . of not being able to contribute to society". "I don't want to live an empty life lying help-lessly in a nursing home for another 30 years," he said. "Life is more than surviving. It's interacting with other people, it's having a family, it's having a career, it's having a wife. It's all of those things and I can't have them. . . . I've tried to figure out other ways but there is none". He came to realize that he would have "to spend the remainder of my life in an institution. . . . What pushed me over the edge was the realization that I was anchored to one spot". "If you're in a situation where you have no freedom," he said, "then you have to make a change, and my change is death".

The truth was that David Rivlin might have enjoyed the life he yearned for, but society blocked his efforts, and government policies forced him into a nursing home. Far more than his physical condition, the system created by public policies robbed him of real choices and, in the end, made his life unendurable. . . .

David Rivlin Would Have Lived If Society Understood True Mercy

The day Rivlin died, Dr. John W. Finn, medical director of the Hospice of Southeastern Michigan, sedated him with Valium and morphine. After that, a person unidentified by the press shut off his ventilator, and David Rivlin died. Hospices were originally founded to comfort terminally ill people. This hospice functioned as a suicide assistance center for a despairing, disabled man. . . .

David Rivlin talked about the limited options that made his life unbearable to him. Sometimes he attributed his confinement to his disability. Advocates of disabled people's so-called "right to die" latched onto those statements as his explanation of why he wanted to die. They ignored the significance of other comments he made. A reporter asked him what he thought of society's view of people with disabilities. "It sucks," Rivlin replied. "Transportation, attitudes, financial help, it's all bad".

Supporters of Rivlin's suicide overlooked such statements. They called his request to die a free and rational choice. The truth was, of course, that his society isolated him. His government aided the nursing home industry in exploiting him for profit. Public policies robbed him of any possibility of a productive and meaningful life. That same system denied him appropriate psychological supports to help him deal with the emotional battering it rained down on him. His freedom and finally his life were stolen by a system that segregated him. In the end, David Rivlin chose the only option left him, and everyone clucked their tongues about how sad it all was.

Analyze the essay:

1. Although David Rivlin chose to end his life, Paul K. Longmore says that his choice was neither free nor rational. Explain what he means by this. Use examples from the text in your answer.

2. Paul K. Longmore is himself disabled. How do you think this fact influences his opinion of whether euthanasia is merciful? Should disabled people view euthanasia differently from nondisabled people? Why or why not?

Euthanasia Threatens Life

Roseanna Cunningham

Roseanna Cunningham is a British politician. In the following essay she argues that euthanasia is a threat to life. She argues that if society legalizes euthanasia, it will be used to kill people whose care has become expensive or burdensome. She points to the Netherlands, where euthanasia is legal, and claims that doctors there have killed their patients without their consent and feel free to suggest death to patients who are facing a bad diagnosis or expensive hospital bill. Rather than trying to legalize euthanasia, Cunningham believes more effort should be put into palliative care—or making people more comfortable as they approach death. But Cunningham says there is no incentive to improve palliative care as long as euthanasia is an option.

Consider the following questions:

1. Why does Cunningham think the elderly should not be viewed as a "problem"?
2. What percent of Dutch doctors have admitted to terminating their patients' lives without their consent, according to Cunningham?
3. In Cunningham's opinion, what is different about legalized euthanasia and "Do Not Resuscitate" orders?

There's an old saying that hard cases make bad law. When it comes to end-of-life decisions, this is never more true. No-one could fail to be moved by some of the very sad stories told about those who beg to be helped

Roseanna Cunningham, "Care, Not Euthanasia, Is the Answer to the 'Problem' of the Elderly," *Times* (London), July 20, 2008, p. 21. Copyright © 2008 Times Newspapers Ltd. Reproduced by permission.

The author believes that more effort should be put into palliative care, care that makes patients more comfortable as death approaches.

to die. Nevertheless, we must question the logic and we must consider the wider impact on society of allowing a change in the law to take place. It is a fundamental shift in what we understand the [United Kingdom] National Health Service to be about.

Caring for the Elderly Is Hard but Must Be Done

This debate is taking place at a very particular moment in our population history. We are frequently presented with demographic research which talks in terms of the "problem" of the increasing number of elderly people in society. This is frequently described as a "burden" on the health service. Caring for them is costly. Challenge the language and it is of course hurriedly amended, but there is a clear implication in the approach and it is that implication which should worry us profoundly. It is only a short jump to applying that same language to individuals. A costly burden and a problem to be solved. It is not only the elderly who would be included in this category because as health professionals and others are quick to point out, the most costly period of a person's life is the last year or two before death, at whatever age that death happens.

Well, here's a truth there's no escaping. We are all going to die. We may be a bit more expensive to maintain in those last months, but that is just as much a part of our healthcare as our earlier years. What we need to do, therefore, is concentrate on doing the things which will make the last months we have as much part of our living as everything that has gone before.

Choose Care, Not Death

Are there some conditions for which palliative care is still difficult to deliver? I'm not a medical expert, but if there are then shouldn't we be seeking ways to research and improve such care until we find solutions? Any bets on the likelihood of that happening while there is another infinitely less expensive option?

And what price further research into the causes, cures and alleviation of the many illnesses of old age, already something of a Cinderella area? The Netherlands is often pointed to as a model for the introduction of assisted suicide as if somehow everything was rosy in the Dutch garden. That is simply not true. Research a few years ago concluded that guidelines there were consistently ignored and almost unenforceable. Half of Dutch doctors felt free to actually suggest euthanasia to their patients and an astonishing

Playing God and Devaluing Life

Might the strongest argument against euthanasia relate not to death but to life? That is, the argument that normalizing it would destroy a sense of the unfathomable mystery of life and seriously damage our human spirit, especially our capacity to find meaning in life.

Margaret Somerville, "The Case Against Euthanasia," *Ottawa Citizen*, June 27, 2008. www.canada.com/ottawacitizen/news/story.html?id = de02045d-51b1-4f4b-aa1a-157f3f79651b.

Palliative Care or Euthanasia?

A 2008 poll in Canada found that people were equally divided on whether they would want to be euthanized or given palliative care at the end of their life. Older Canadians favored palliative care.

Question: "At the end of your life, what would you choose—palliative care or euthanasia?"

General Population

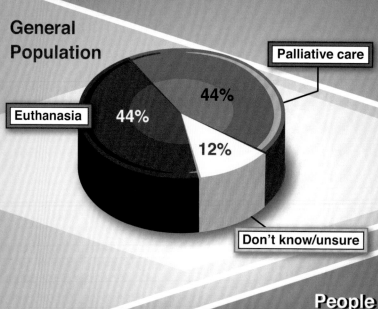

Palliative care 44%

Euthanasia 44%

12%

Don't know/unsure

People Aged 60 and Over

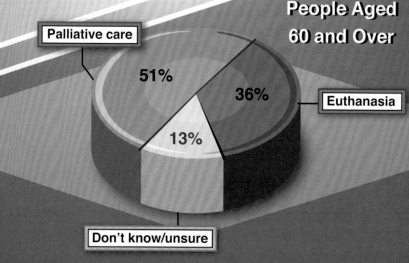

Palliative care 51%

Euthanasia 36%

13%

Don't know/unsure

Taken from: Focus Canada, September 24–October 21, 2008.

25% revealed anonymously that they had terminated patients' lives without an overt request.

As an example, the same study refers to the case of a Dutch nun "helpfully" euthanised by her doctor who decided that her religious scruples prevented her making what he felt would be the most sensible and entirely justified decision. There are many other such cases that point to flaws in the Dutch system that can't be ignored. An examination of the reality in Oregon, the only US state to adopt this legal change[1], reveals a similar story of confusion and dubious decisions.

A Dignified Death Is an Unforced One

Dignity in dying is important. That is why we already accept that sometimes it is right to stand back and allow nature to take its course. There can be few families who have not, at some stage, had to respond to a hospital request for guidance on whether "Do Not Resuscitate" should be entered into a patient's notes. The discontinuation of painful and pointless medical intervention that will only be effective for a short time is, however, not the same thing as actively intervening to help nature along. Omission and commission are not the same in this context and to suggest they are is to be deliberately and dangerously misleading.

But what about the doctors in this country who have already taken the decision to help some patients die? We know that it happens and there is a case in the news right now involving a doctor charged with prescribing sleeping pills to a patient who said she wanted to end her life. The fact that it might already happen, however, does not provide an argument for legalising euthanasia. Once you do that, the exceptional becomes routine.

Society Suffers When Euthanasia Is Legal

Growing numbers of health professionals are invoking the conscience opt-out provided in the abortion legisla-

1. In 2008 the state of Washington legalized assisted suicide.

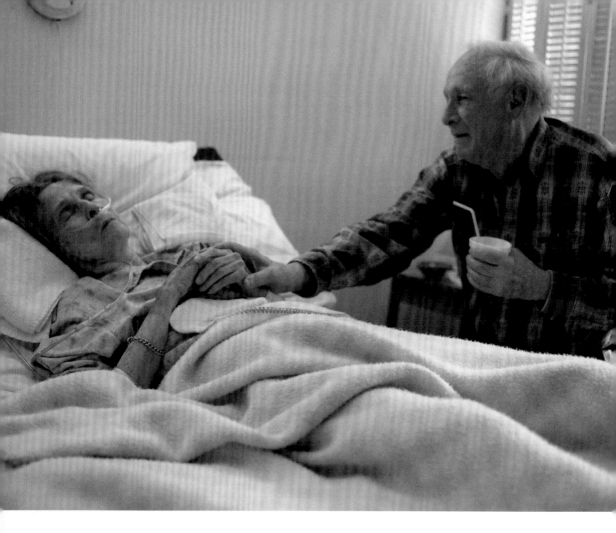

The author stresses that dignity in dying is important to families and that one should let nature take its course.

tion and there is already a challenge to that in the House of Commons. Increasingly, "conscience" is being derided and sidelined and those who do want to rely on it are having their views dismissed. How much more sharp would that become if we introduce assisted suicide?

We as patients, the medical profession and society as a whole all stand to lose if this becomes the norm. Instead, I would prefer to see us demand better services for the elderly and the dying, services which recognise the needs of the whole individual—medical, physical, spiritual. Let's put our money where our mouths are and alleviate the fears and concerns of . . . all those who may be worried about the future. That's a far better way for society to go.

Analyze the essay:

1. One of Cunningham's key arguments is her claim that there is no reason for health-care providers to get better at taking care of people as long as euthanasia is legal. Do you agree with this claim? Why or why not?

2. In this essay the author suggests that euthanasia threatens all life. What do you think? Can euthanasia exist as an appropriate option for some people without threatening the lives of others? Explain your position.

Euthanasia Respects Life

Robert Lake

In the following essay Robert Lake argues that euthanasia does not devalue life. He claims that it is unlikely that euthanasia would be used except only when appropriate, and in these cases it could help relieve suffering. In his opinion, relieving suffering is an act that is respectful of life because it reflects how much people value it. He also points out that legalizing euthanasia would regulate it. As a regulated, legal practice, standards and protocols would be developed to ensure that no one is exploited or forced into euthanasia, which helps keep people safe. Finally, Lake says that forms of euthanasia are legal in several nations, but no evidence suggests that these nations have any less respect for human life than countries without legalized euthanasia. For all these reasons he concludes that euthanasia is a safe practice that respects the enormity of both life and death.

Lake is a Canadian journalist and a retired professor of psychology.

Consider the following questions:
1. How might legalizing euthanasia make people more likely to seek medical treatment, according to Lake?
2. How might legalizing euthanasia actually prolong life, in Lake's opinion?
3. What, in Lake's opinion, is human life? What kind of human life does he say is worth living?

In a recent [Ottawa (ON)] *Citizen* article opposing assisted suicide, ethicist Margaret Somerville, too harshly criticizes her teaching ability and, in passing, perhaps unfairly slams the media.

Prof. Somerville teaches an ethics course at McGill [University]; part of that course covers her arguments against euthanasia, which she regrets fail to convince her students. In an e-mail to them she apologized for ineffective teaching.

After reading the reasons why Prof. Somerville opposes euthanasia, my guess is Prof. Somerville's teaching is fine; it's her arguments that wobble.

Euthanasia Does Not Overexpose Us to Death

She also blames the media for her students' reluctance to accept her reasoning, writing, "the vast exposure to death that we are subjected to in both current-affairs and entertainment programs might have overwhelmed our sensitivity to the awesomeness of death and, likewise, of inflicting it."

Demonstrators in Rome, Italy, march in support of right-to-die legislation. Many countries in Europe now have euthanasia laws.

Americans Want Options for Death

An annual Gallup poll consistently finds that most Americans are in favor of legalizing some form of physician-assisted death.

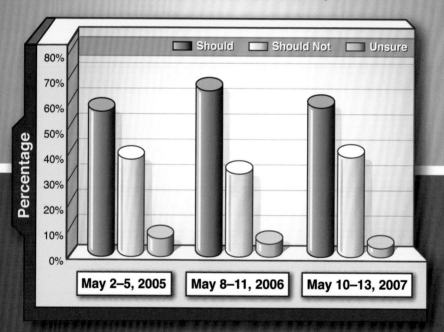

"When a person has a disease that cannot be cured and is living in severe pain, do you think doctors should or should not be allowed by law to assist the patient to commit suicide if the patient requests it?"

Taken from: Gallup poll, May 10–13, 2007.

I'm not convinced that media "vastly expose" us to death, but past generations attended public hangings and bear baitings, surely "entertainment programs" likely to overwhelm sensitivity. I suspect contemporary North American society is more sensitive to death than previously: for instance, Americans are shocked by military deaths in Iraq that would have been regarded as puny during the Second World War.

Obviously, a newspaper article doesn't permit Prof. Somerville to outline her arguments as fully as in class or in her book *Death Talk: The Case Against Euthanasia and Physician-Assisted Suicide*, but let's examine her arguments, remembering that an article doesn't permit me space for elaboration either.

Legal Euthanasia Protects People from Harm

a) *Euthanasia would harm both law and medicine.* Why? Surely, it would alter them, making legal practices which are not legal now. But harm? I don't see that legalizing abortion, once a backroom practice, harmed either law or medicine. In fact, legal and safe abortions may increase women's respect for the law. Legal euthanasia may prevent suffering people searching for end runs around the law.

b) *Euthanasia may make people less likely to seek medical treatment.* Possibly, but I suggest it may make people more likely to seek treatment, knowing doctors have one more technique, albeit dreadful, in their arsenal for alleviating suffering.

c) *It's wrong to kill another human.* It certainly is, but that argument pursued zealously means we should disband the Canadian Armed Forces. Regrettably, armies sooner or later kill. Regrettably, police do too. We hope they do reluctantly and rarely, but we sanction their killings.

Euthanasia Does Not Devalue Life

d) *Euthanasia would necessarily cause loss of respect for human life.* Is there any evidence that jurisdictions such as the Netherlands which have experimented with euthanasia have less respect for human life than, say, the United States? Or Canada? This argument also raises the question: what is "human life," which I'll return to.

e) *It would open up the slippery slope and set precedents that would present serious dangers to future generations.* This threadbare argument is always pulled from the hat when others fail. Any course of action opens up opportunities and dangers. Will drastically reducing carbon emissions wreck the economy or save future generations from climatic catastrophe? Or both? Or neither? Take bold action or sit on our hands, both create opportunities and problems for future generations. That's life.

f) *Recognizing death as an acceptable way to relieve suffering could influence people contemplating suicide.* Sure could. I presume Prof. Somerville fears it would nudge people in the direction of suicide. Why? Possibly, it would nudge people in the direction of seeking help. Not everyone who considers assisted suicide goes ahead.

Regulating Euthanasia Keeps It Safe

Perhaps the strongest argument for legalizing assisted suicide is that, as more of our citizens are elderly, continued prohibition may create the dangerous situation that exists in some Latin American countries where hospitals are flooded with women whose illegal abortions have been botched. Already, Germans, in small numbers now, cross the border to Switzerland to seek assisted suicides. Prohibition didn't work with booze or abortions. Regulating euthanasia sounds dreadful, but it may prevent desperate people grievously maiming themselves by going it alone or aided by quacks.

This brings me to two final points I must deal with far too quickly. I suspect legalizing assisted-suicide on average will prolong life. Why? The chief fear of people with terminal diseases and aging people, I believe, is the fear of losing control. This may be particularly true the more competent a person has been. A decades-

Dying with Dignity

When our beloved old cat had to be put down because he was in unbearable pain and had no quality of life, the whole family mourned his passing. But we knew it would have been cruel and selfish of us to keep him alive. . . . Surely people suffering the torments of hell from cancer, MS, Parkinson's or motor neurone disease should be given the same compassion. Isn't their right to die with dignity more valid than that of a pet, no matter how well loved?

Lorraine Kelly, "We All Deserve Right to Die with Dignity," *Sun* (UK), December 13, 2008.

old psychological experiment showed that loud noise interfered with people's ability to perform tasks. But, if the people believed they could turn off the noise they performed normally, even as the noise continued. Your neighbour's loud music is irritating but yours isn't. Knowing assisted suicide is available may give suffering people a sense of control. Their suffering can be terminated when they choose. Often they'll choose to continue listening to life's music if they control the volume.

The building housing the German branch office of the Swiss euthanasia organization in Hanover is shown. Many Germans have turned to the Swiss for assisted suicide.

Life Is Subjective—and So Is Death

And this brings us to the question that neither Prof. Somerville nor I nor you nor anybody can satisfactorily answer. What is "human life"? If we could definitely answer that, there would be no abortion debate. We'd know precisely when human life begins and possibly when it ends. We'd know if "brain dead" is the end of "human life." We would know if Socrates was right or being pompous when he said, "The unexamined life isn't worth living." We all know what human life is, except we all know something different.

So, kudos for Prof. Somerville for trying to convince her students, but more kudos to them for not buckling under to the professorial line.

Analyze the essay:

1. Lake argues that if euthanasia were legalized it would be regulated, which would help keep it safe. This argument—that legalizing a practice gets its use out in the open—is also made regarding drugs, abortion, and other topics. What do you think— is legalizing a controversial practice a good way to keep it safe? Or does legalizing a controversial practice dangerously encourage it? Explain your reasoning.

2. Lake says there is no reason to think that legalizing euthanasia will set society on a "slippery slope" to abuse it. How do you think each of the authors in this section would respond to this claim? Write one sentence for each author.

Section Two:
Model Essays
and Writing
Exercises

The Five-Paragraph Essay

An *essay* is a short piece of writing that discusses or analyzes one topic. The five-paragraph essay is a form commonly used in school assignments and tests. Every five-paragraph essay begins with an *introduction*, ends with a *conclusion*, and features three *supporting paragraphs* in the middle.

The Thesis Statement. The introduction includes the essay's thesis statement. The thesis statement presents the argument or point the author is trying to make about the topic. The essays in this book all have different thesis statements because they are making different arguments about euthanasia. The thesis statement should clearly tell the reader what the essay will be about. A focused thesis statement helps determine what will be in the essay; the subsequent paragraphs are spent developing and supporting its argument.

The Introduction. In addition to presenting the thesis statement, a well-written introductory paragraph captures the attention of the reader and explains why the topic being explored is important. It may provide the reader with background information on the subject matter or feature an anecdote that illustrates a point relevant to the topic. It could also present startling information that clarifies the point of the essay or puts forth a contradictory position that the essay will refute. Further techniques for writing an introduction are found later in this section.

The Supporting Paragraphs. The introduction is then followed by three (or more) supporting paragraphs. These are the main body of the essay. Each paragraph presents and develops a *subtopic* that supports the essay's thesis statement. Each subtopic is spearheaded by a *topic sentence* and supported by its own facts, details, and examples. The writer can use various kinds of supporting material and details to back up the topic of each supporting paragraph. These may include statistics, quotations from people with special knowledge or expertise, historic facts, and anecdotes. A rule of writing is that specific and concrete examples are more convincing than vague, general, or unsupported assertions.

The Conclusion. The conclusion is the paragraph that closes the essay. Its function is to summarize or reiterate the main idea of the essay. It may recall an idea from the introduction or briefly examine the larger implications of the thesis. Because the conclusion is also the last chance a writer has to make an impression on the reader, it is important that it not simply repeat what has been presented elsewhere in the essay but close it in a clear, final, and memorable way.

Although the order of the essay's component paragraphs is important, they do not have to be written in the order presented here. Some writers like to decide on a thesis and write the introduction paragraph first. Other writers like to focus first on the body of the essay and write the introduction and conclusion later.

Pitfalls to Avoid

When writing essays about controversial issues such as euthanasia, it is important to remember that disputes over the material are common precisely because there are many different perspectives. Remember to state your arguments in careful and measured terms. Evaluate your topic fairly—avoid overstating negative qualities of one perspective or understating positive qualities of another. Use examples, facts, and details to support any assertions you make.

The Persuasive Essay

There are many types of essays, but in general, they are usually short compositions in which the writer expresses and discusses an opinion about something. In the persuasive essay the writer tries to persuade (convince) the reader to do something or to agree with the writer's opinion about something. Examples of persuasive writing are easy to find. Advertising is one common example. Through commercial and print ads, companies try to convince the public to buy their products for specific reasons. Much everyday writing is persuasive, too. Letters to the editor, posts from sports fans on team Web sites, even handwritten notes urging a friend to listen to a new CD—all are examples of persuasive writing.

The Tools of Persuasion

The writer of the persuasive essay uses various tools to persuade the reader. Here are some of them:

Facts and Statistics. A fact is a statement that no one, typically, would disagree with. It can be verified by information in reputable resources, such as encyclopedias, almanacs, government Web sites, or reference books about the topic of the fact.

Examples of Facts and Statistics

Christmas is celebrated on December 25.

Berlin is the capital of Germany.

Twenty percent of all pregnancies end in miscarriage.

According to an ABC News/*Washington Post* poll, 74 percent of Americans believe the United States is not doing enough to prevent illegal aliens from entering the country.

It is important to note that facts and statistics can be *misstated* (written down or quoted incorrectly), *misinterpreted* (not understood correctly by the user), or *misused* (not used fairly). But if a writer uses facts and statistics properly, they can add authority to the writer's essay.

Opinions. An opinion is what a person thinks about something. It can be contested or argued with. However, opinions of people who are experts on the topic or who have personal experience are often very convincing. Many persuasive essays are written to convince the reader that the writer's opinion is worth believing and acting on.

Testimonials. A testimonial is a statement given by a person who is thought to be an expert or who has another trait people admire, such as being a celebrity. Television commercials frequently use testimonials to convince watchers to buy the products they are advertising.

Examples. An example is something that is representative of a group or type ("Labrador retriever" is an example of the group "dog"). Examples are used to help define, describe, or illustrate something to make it more understandable.

Anecdotes. Anecdotes are extended examples. They are little stories with a beginning, middle, and end. They can be used just like examples to explain something or to show something about a topic.

Appeals to Reason. One way to convince readers that an opinion or action is right is to appeal to reason or logic. This often revolves around the idea that if some ideas are true, another must also be true. Here is an example of one type of appeal to reason:
  – Not every person who drinks becomes an alcoholic. In the same way, not every person who smokes marijuana will become dependent on it. For this reason, marijuana should, like alcohol, be legalized.

Appeals to emotion. Another way to persuade readers to believe or do something is to appeal to their emotions—love, fear, pity, loyalty, and anger are some of the emotions to which writers appeal. A writer who wants to persuade someone not to eat meat might appeal to their love of animals:

- If you own a cat, dog, hamster, or bird, you should not eat meat. It makes no sense to pamper and love your pet while at the same time supporting the merciless slaughter of other animals for your dinner.

Ridicule and Name-Calling. Ridicule and name-calling are not good techniques to use in a persuasive essay. Instead of exploring the strengths of the topic, the writer who uses these relies on making those who oppose the main idea look foolish, evil, or stupid. In most cases, the writer who does this weakens the argument.

Bandwagon. The writer who uses the bandwagon technique uses the idea that "everybody thinks this or is doing this; therefore it is valid." The bandwagon method is not a very authoritative way to convince your reader of your point.

Words and Phrases Common to Persuasive Essays

accordingly	it stands to reason
because	it then follows that
consequently	obviously
clearly	since
for this reason	subsequently
indeed	therefore
it is necessary to	this is why
it makes sense to	thus
it seems clear that	we must

Would Euthanasia Put Society on a Slippery Slope?

Editor's Notes A common argument made about euthanasia is that it puts society on a slippery slope to accept even more harmful practices, such as the killing of not only sick people, but undesirable or unpopular people. The following model essay explores the arguments for and against the "slippery slope" argument against euthanasia. After explaining the position of each side, the author explains why she believes that euthanasia does not in fact put society on a slippery slope toward more evil practices.

The notes in the margin point out key features of the essay and will help you understand how the essay is organized. Also note that all sources are cited using Modern Language Association (MLA) style.* For more information on how to cite your sources, see Appendix C. In addition, consider the following:

1. How does the introduction engage the reader's attention?
2. What persuasive techniques are used in the essay?
3. What purpose do the essay's quotes serve?
4. Does the essay convince you of its point?

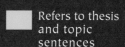 Refers to thesis and topic sentences

 Refers to supporting details

Paragraph 1

Euthanasia is one of several social issues that generate controversy not necessarily because of what happens when it is practiced, but because of what *else* might happen if it becomes commonplace. This type of reasoning is called "slippery slope" or "floodgates" logic, meaning

---

* Editor's Note: In applying MLA style guidelines in this book, the following simplifications have been made: Parenthetical text citations are confined to direct quotations only; electronic source documentation in the Works Cited list omits date of access, page ranges, and some detailed facts of publication.

63

that if a particular practice or behavior becomes routine, it could encourage even more harmful behaviors and practices to occur. While it is scary to think that the regular use of euthanasia would in fact put society on a slippery slope to accepting more harmful practices, all signs indicate there would be no consequences beyond euthanasia than the relief of suffering of terminally ill people.

This is the essay's thesis statement. It tells the reader what will be argued in the following paragraphs.

Paragraph 2

Opponents of euthanasia warn that becoming too comfortable with ending life will result in needless tragedies—like what happened in New Orleans during Hurricane Katrina, when medical workers caused the deaths of four people as their hospital became flooded and cut off from electricity. The workers said they acted out of an instinct to relieve their patients' suffering—yet it is very likely that had the patients not been killed, they would have lived through the crisis. That's why, according to Dr. John Burns, "the specter of physicians accepting the veterinary ethic of dispensing death to end suffering ought to scare the 'heck' out of us" (13). Burns and others see the disabled, the elderly, and even minorities as those who might one day be viewed as deserving of euthanasia if society accepts the practice in any form.

This is the topic sentence of Paragraph 2. It is a subset of the essay's thesis. It tells what specific point this paragraph will make.

This quote is a supporting detail of Paragraph 2. It helps support the point the author is making.

Paragraph 3

Others, however, reject this perspective, viewing it as a hysterical tactic used to scare people into not taking any action at all. Paul Heslin, an Irish physician, is one of many who reject the suggestion that euthanasia will lead society to commit more harmful, hideous acts. "We have no fear that owners or vets killing their pets or horses, when this is the practical thing to do, will lead to widespread killing of pets," says Heslin. "There's no fear of floodgates when it comes to animals" (16). Indeed, euthanizing cats, dogs, and other pets when they become too old or ill to maintain a certain quality of life

This quote was taken from Viewpoint 2. When you see particularly striking quotes, save them to use to support points in your essays.

is accepted throughout the United States, but nowhere has it led to the arbitrary or wholesale killing of animals. Heslin and others argue that such an argument is fear-mongering used to suppress and discourage solutions to difficult social problems.

Paragraph 4

While the concerns of those who warn of a slippery slope are understandable, they do not hold water in the long run. As Heslin notes, there are plenty of areas in which Americans accept one type of behavior without feeling compelled to extend it to other situations. Allowing people to drink alcohol does not put the majority of Americans on the path to becoming alcoholics; allowing people to marry someone of a different race or religion does not set society on a slope to accepting the marriage of people to animals, or marriage between multiple groups of people. Such fears are hysterical and unwarranted. A 2005 Pew Research Center survey shows that the majority of Americans agree: 70 percent of them said they think that there are circumstances in which a patient should sometimes be allowed to die. Furthermore, 74 percent said in cases in which a dying patient has not expressed his wishes in advance, and is unable to communicate his wishes, a family member should be allowed to make the decision whether or not to continue medical care. Clearly, these Americans are not concerned that allowing some people to die in the face of suffering will open the door to abuse or murder.

This is the topic sentence of Paragraph 4. Note that all of the paragraph's details fit with it—or, *support* it.

This statistic helps support the paragraph's main idea: that Americans do not think euthanasia is a threatening practice. Only use facts, quotes, statistics, and anecdotes that clearly and directly support your arguments.

Paragraph 5

Americans should realize that if they support euthanasia, they are giving their approval to ending the suffering of the terminally ill—nothing more, nothing less. They should not fear that somehow their support of this humane practice will lead to Holocaust-style extermination camps or the wholesale slaughter of anyone over the age of seventy. That's letting our

This sentence serves to wrap up what the essay has discussed—but note how it does so without repeating every point that was made.

worst fears get away from us—an understandable yet unproductive response to life's most serious questions and problems.

Works Cited

Burns, John. "The Veterinary Ethic." *New American* 21 Aug. 2006: 13.

Heslin, Paul. "Language Hides the Realities of Death." *Irish Medical Times* 1 Aug. 2008: 16.

Exercise 1A: Create an Outline from an Existing Essay

It often helps to create an outline of the five-paragraph essay before you write it. The outline can help you organize the information, arguments, and evidence you have gathered during your research.

For this exercise, create an outline that could have been used to write "Would Euthanasia Put Society on a Slippery Slope?" This "reverse engineering" exercise is meant to help familiarize you with how outlines can help classify and arrange information.

To do this you will need to
    1. articulate the essay's thesis,
    2. pinpoint important pieces of evidence,
    3. flag quotes that supported the essay's ideas, and
    4. identify key points that supported the argument.

Part of the outline has already been started to give you an idea of the assignment.

Outline
I. Paragraph 1
Write the essay's thesis:

II. Paragraph 2
Topic:

    Supporting Detail i. Example of how four people were killed by medical workers during Hurricane Katrina in New Orleans.

III. Paragraph 3
Topic: Supporters of euthanasia do not worry that it will put society on a slippery slope to more nefarious practices—they view this suggestion as a hysterical tactic used to scare people.

Supporting Detail i.

Supporting Detail ii.

IV. Paragraph 4
Topic:

Supporting Detail i. Rationale that legalizing other provocative behaviors has not led to the abuse or escalation of them.
Supporting Detail ii. Statistics about how many Americans support euthanasia.

V. Paragraph 5:
Write the essay's conclusion:

Exercise 1B: Create an Outline for Your Own Essay

The model essay you just read expresses a particular point of view about euthanasia. For this exercise, your assignment is to find supporting ideas, choose specific and concrete details, create an outline, and ultimately write a five-paragraph essay making a different, or even opposing, point about euthanasia. Your goal is to use persuasive techniques to convince your reader.

Part l: Write a thesis statement.

The following thesis statement would be appropriate for an opposing essay on why euthanasia puts society on a slippery slope:

Once we allow one group of people to be killed to relieve their suffering (the terminally ill), there is nothing to stop us from designating other groups of people who should receive the same service—such as the severely disabled, the comatose, the old, the retarded, or even babies born with birth defects.

Or see the sample paper topics suggested in Appendix D for more ideas.

Part II: Brainstorm pieces of supporting evidence.

Using information from some of the viewpoints in the previous section and from the information found in Section Three of this book, write down three arguments or pieces of evidence that support the thesis statement you selected. Then, for each of these three arguments, write down supportive facts, examples, and details that support it. These could be:

- statistical information
- personal memories and anecdotes
- quotes from experts, peers, or family members
- observations of people's actions and behaviors
- specific and concrete details

Supporting pieces of evidence for the above sample thesis statement are found in this book and include:

- The Alfred Mohler quote in the box accompanying Viewpoint One: *"The 'slippery slope' argument is neither fallacious nor irrelevant, as recent developments in the Netherlands have made graphically clear. Once doctors are allowed to choose death over life, the resulting Culture of Death will inevitably discount human life in other contexts as well."* Albert Mohler, "Euthanasia for Newborns— Killing in the Netherlands," AlbertMohler.com, March 14, 2005. www.albertmohler.com/commentary_read .php?cdate = 2005-03-14.
- The story of David Rivlin told in Viewpoint Four by Paul K. Longmore.

- Statistic in Viewpoint Five about how 25 percent of doctors in the Netherlands—where euthanasia is regularly practiced—have ended their patients' lives without their request or permission.
- Chart accompanying Viewpoint Five showing that 44 percent of Canadians are interested in receiving palliative care—care that keeps a terminally ill person comfortable until they die naturally.

Part III: Place the information from Part I in outline form.

Part IV: Write the arguments or supporting statements in paragraph form.

By now you have three arguments that support the paragraph's thesis statement, as well as supporting material. Use the outline to write out your three supporting arguments in paragraph form. Make sure each paragraph has a topic sentence that states the paragraph's thesis clearly and broadly. Then, add supporting sentences that express the facts, quotes, details, and examples that support the paragraph's argument. The paragraph may also have a concluding or summary sentence.

Euthanasia Is Humane

Essay Two

Editor's Notes The following model essay argues that euthanasia offers people a merciful, dignified end when they are suffering from a terminal disease. Like the first model essay, this essay is structured as a five-paragraph persuasive essay in which each paragraph contributes a supporting piece of evidence to develop the argument. Each supporting paragraph explores one of three distinct reasons why the author believes euthanasia is merciful.

As you read this essay, take note of its components and how they are organized (the sidebars in the margins provide further explanation).

■ Refers to thesis and topic sentences

■ Refers to supporting details

Paragraph 1

Terminally ill people rarely die swiftly or comfortably. Their death is usually a prolonged experience that leaves them in excruciating pain, unaware of their surroundings, and dependent on others for life's basic needs and functions. After a dignified, meaningful life, many humans become prisoners trapped in their disintegrating minds and bodies. Euthanasia offers such people the chance to die a swift, compassionate, and dignified death. In this way, euthanasia—which comes from a Greek word that means "good death," or "dying well"—should be viewed as a moral, merciful act that relieves suffering and honors life.

The essay begins with specific, descriptive details meant to grab your attention.

This is the essay's thesis statement. It tells what main point the essay will argue.

Paragraph 2

Euthanasia seems especially merciful when we consider the awfulness that surrounds the end of life. According to the Rand Corporation, 40 percent of American deaths are preceded by a ten-year period of dementia, confusion, and severe weakness. No one wants to cap off a dignified life of accomplishment and meaning by being unable to go to the bathroom alone or being unable to recognize family members. Americans should be willing in such situations

This is a *supporting detail*. This information directly supports the topic sentence, helping to prove it true.

What is the topic sentence of Paragraph 2? How did you recognize it?

71

to treat our loved ones with as much sympathy and care as we do our pets, which we put out of their misery when they pass the point of comfort. When a pet reaches this painful point, we graciously help them toward life's end rather than force them to tough it out on their own. As Doctor Paul Heslin has put it: "We put our pets down when we want to save them suffering. We keep our patients alive despite our occasional failure to keep severe pain at bay and their calls for peace." (16) Heslin argues that a veterinarian should be among the few people who help determine a person's end, because of the vet's "pragmatic approach to quality-of-life issues." (16) Surely we can show the same compassion and care to ending the suffering of our loved ones as we do for our loyal pets.

Why has the author included Paul Heslin's job title?

Paragraph 3

Further proving that euthanasia is merciful is the way it fits with a doctor's responsibility to his or her patients' needs. Obviously, a doctor's job is not solely to make sick people healthy. Sometimes people are so ill they can't be cured. At this point, a doctor's job turns from being a healer to one of a pain reliever. In caring for the terminally ill, many doctors agree that the most humane course of treatment is no treatment at all, but a relief from suffering and pain. Euthanasia is an important part of this course of action. For example, a 2003 poll by the Voluntary Euthanasia Society (VES), a pro-euthanasia group in Britain, found that 55 percent of that country's physicians supported at least some form of euthanasia. More recently, a 2007 poll of more than one thousand doctors, conducted by the New York–based Louis Finkelstein Institute, found that 57 percent of doctors think it is ethical to assist an individual who, due to unbearable suffering, has made a rational choice to die. This is why, according to medical ethics professors Len Doyal and Lesley Doyal, "Doctors should be able to withdraw life sustaining treatment when they intend to accelerate death as well as to relieve suffering" (1,079). When looked at through the lens of pain relief and suffering, it becomes clear that euthanasia is actually a

"Obviously," "At this point," and "For example" are all transitional phrases that keep the ideas flowing. See Preface B for a list of such words commonly found in persuasive essays.

Analyze this quote. What do you think made the author want to select it for inclusion in the essay?

critical part of end-of-life care. Only a cruel person would want their loved one to suffer unnecessarily.

Paragraph 4

The morality and mercifulness of euthanasia is further evidenced by America's overwhelming support for it. In 2007, for example, an Associated Press–Ipsos poll found that 68 percent of Americans said there are sometimes circumstances in which a patient should be allowed to die. These results were confirmed by a Pew Research Center poll in which 74 percent of Americans said that if a patient with a terminal disease is unable to communicate and has not made his or her own wishes known in advance, the closest family member should be allowed to decide whether to continue medical treatment. Finally, the same poll found that an overwhelming 84 percent of Americans approve of laws that let patients decide whether or not they want to be kept alive through medical treatment. These numbers represent very high levels of support for causing death under the right circumstances and should cause other Americans to realize that euthanasia is very often a humane option at the end of life.

These statistics were taken from Appendix A in this book and put in narrative form. This book contains many resources for writing an essay on euthanasia.

Paragraph 5

Because death is so final and sad, there can be perhaps no truly "good death"—but some deaths are better than others, and euthanasia is the key to distinguishing between them. We can help our loved ones die better and more peacefully by not forcing them to needlessly suffer once death has closed in upon them. This is why euthanasia must be regarded as a humane, merciful act that offers dignity and compassion at life's cruel end.

Works Cited

Doyal, Len, and Lesley Doyal. "Why Active Euthanasia and Physician Assisted Suicide Should Be Legalized." *British Medical Journal* 323 (10 Nov. 2001): 1079.

Heslin, Paul. "Language Hides the Realities of Death." *Irish Medical Times* 31 Jul. 2008: 16. < http://www.imt.ie/opinion/2008/07/language_hides_the_realities_o.html > .

Exercise 2A: Create an Outline from an Existing Essay

As you did for the first model essay in this section, create an outline that could have been used to write "Euthanasia Is Humane." Be sure to identify the essay's thesis statement, its supporting ideas, its descriptive passages, and key pieces of evidence that were used.

Exercise 2B: Identify Persuasive Techniques

Essayists use many techniques to persuade you to agree with their ideas or to do something they want you to do. Some of the most common techniques are described in Preface B of this section, "The Persuasive Essay." These tools are facts and statistics, opinions, testimonials, examples and anecdotes, appeals to reason, appeals to emotion, ridicule and name-calling, and bandwagon. Go back to the preface and review these tools. Remember that most of these tools can be used to enhance your essay, but some of them—particularly ridiculing, name-calling, and bandwagon—can detract from the essay's effectiveness. Nevertheless, you should be able to recognize them in the essays you read.

Some writers use one persuasive tool throughout their whole essay. For example, the essay may be one extended anecdote, or the writer may rely entirely on statistics. But most writers typically use a combination of persuasive tools. Essay Two, "Euthanasia Is Humane," does this.

Problem One
Read Essay Two again and see if you can find every persuasive tool used. Put that information in the following table. Part of the table is filled in for you. Explanatory notes appear after the table. (NOTE: You will not fill in every box. No paragraph contains all of the techniques.)

	Paragraph 1 Sentence #	Paragraph 2 Sentence #	Paragraph 3 Sentence #	Paragraph 4 Sentence #	Paragraph 5 Sentence #
Fact					
Statistic		2[a]			
Opinion	1[b]				
Testimonial					
Example					
Anecdote					
Appeal to Reason		8[c]			
Appeal to Emotion					
Ridicule					
Name-Calling			11[d]		
Bandwagon				5[e]	

Notes

a. That 40 percent of American deaths are preceded by a ten-year period of dementia, confusion, and severe weakness is a statistic.
b. That euthanasia is merciful is the author's opinion.
c. The author appeals to reason when she argues that Americans should offer euthanasia to their family members if they love them as much as they do their pets.
d. When the author calls people who oppose euthanasia "cruel" she is ridiculing them. This is probably not the best way of getting her point across.
e. When the author tells Americans they should approve of euthanasia just because other Americans do, she is encouraging them to jump on the bandwagon of public opinion.

Now, look at the table you have produced. Which persuasive tools does this essay rely on most heavily? Which are not used at all?

Problem Two
Apply this exercise to the other model essays in this section, and the viewpoints in Section One, when you are finished reading them.

Euthanasia Threatens the Disabled

Editor's Notes   The final model essay argues that euthanasia threatens the disabled. Supported by facts, quotes, statistics, and opinions, it tries to persuade the reader that the existence of euthanasia poses a threat to disabled Americans by pressuring them to end their lives for financial, emotional, and other reasons.

This essay differs from the previous model essays in that it is longer than five paragraphs. Sometimes five paragraphs are simply not enough to adequately develop an idea. Extending the length of an essay can allow the reader to explore a topic in more depth or present multiple pieces of evidence that together provide a complete picture of a topic. Longer essays can also help readers discover the complexity of a subject by examining a topic beyond its superficial exterior. Moreover, the ability to write a sustained research or position paper is a valuable skill you will need as you advance academically.

As you read, consider the questions posed in the margins. Continue to identify thesis statements, supporting details, transitions, and quotations. Examine the introductory and concluding paragraphs to understand how they give shape to the essay. Finally, evaluate the essay's general structure and assess its overall effectiveness.

▢ Refers to thesis and topic sentences

▢ Refers to supporting details

Paragraph 1

Although euthanasia is in theory supposed to be received only by the dying, once it becomes accepted, who is eligible for the practice could be dangerously expanded to include the disabled—which, according to the U.S. Census Bureau, includes 49.7 million people, or nearly one in five Americans. This is why some of the most vocal opponents of euthanasia are disabled people: They and their families rightly argue the practice puts them in jeopardy by

What is the essay's thesis statement? How did you recognize it?

encouraging the killing of, rather than the care of, people who are handicapped.

Paragraph 2

Opponents of euthanasia think that making death an option for the severely disabled is a way of pressuring them to save their families the high cost of their care. In truth, it is very expensive to care for disabled Americans—many need twenty-four-hour care and require expensive equipment, multiple prescriptions, and the help of live-in nurses and other caregivers. Very few Americans can afford such treatment and thus fear euthanasia will be unfairly presented to the disabled as a cost-saving option. As quadriplegic Richard Radtke has explained, "There is a big fear of being a burden on family finances, society, the world. Feeling like a burden on your family and friends is devastating." Radtke and others worry that, out of concern for their families, disabled people will choose death over life. For this reason, he thinks greater effort should be put into making care for the disabled more affordable. "Our efforts should focus on making our communities more responsive to those who need help to live, rather than figuring out these policies to help people die" (61).

Paragraph 3

Radtke and others also fear they could potentially be pushed towards death by those who view disabled lives as too restrictive or agonizing to be worth living. Often, when confronted with disability, many nondisabled Americans think, "If that happened to me I would die," or, "I could never survive such an awful thing." Many even think, "I'd rather be dead than paralyzed." This type of thinking was reflected in a study reported in the *Annals of Emergency Medicine*, which found that although 86 percent of quadriplegics rated their quality of life as average or better than average, only 17 percent of their medical staff thought so. Said Larry McAfee, a disabled Georgia man, "You're looked upon as a second-rate citizen" (qtd. in Longmore 46). Such judgments are an outrage. Just

Make a list of everyone quoted in this essay. What types of people have been quoted? What makes them qualified to speak on this topic?

What is the topic sentence of Paragraph 3? What pieces of evidence are used to show that it is true?

because a disabled person's life is governed by a different set of routines and relationships does not mean their life is any less satisfying, meaningful, or precious—but accepting euthanasia implies otherwise.

Paragraph 4

Euthanasia also threatens the disabled when it is presented as a viable option for ending what could otherwise be a satisfying, fulfilling life. There is perhaps no better example of this than Radtke, a professor at the University of Hawaii. Radtke is paralyzed from the neck down, and as a result he is unable to clean, feed, or dress himself without help. Despite his disability, Radtke has lived a full and productive life: He is the author of more than seventy papers and the founder of a disability rights organization. He runs a camp for disabled youth and cares and provides for his wife and daughter. Radtke uses his own life as an example of how offering euthanasia to the disabled threatens to extinguish the richness they might offer themselves, their families, and their communities. "It is difficult when we encounter disability to see clearly what is possible and where life is going to take us," he says. But euthanasia will cause America to "lose a lot of people who can make a difference. We cannot even dream of what those losses might be right now" (59–60). Radtke and other disabled people deserve to be presented with more creative options for how to live instead of being presented with options for death.

> What pieces of this essay are opinions? What parts are facts? Make a list of opinions and facts, and see which the author relies on more.

Paragraph 5

Another way in which the availability of euthanasia threatens the disabled is when it is used to tacitly convince people they would be better off dead. This is what happened to David Rivlin, another quadriplegic who, after a swimming accident, was confined to a dreadfully repressive assisted living facility. Paul K. Longmore has documented the tragic demise of Rivlin, who petitioned a Michigan court to let him die by disconnecting the ventilator on which he relied for breathing. Although Rivlin made the request

> What is the topic sentence of Paragraph 5?

to die, Longmore believes he was pushed to seek death when all other avenues of living became too burdensome, expensive, or unbearable. "Supporters of Rivlin's [death] called his request to die a free and rational choice," says Longmore. "The truth was, of course, that his society isolated him. His government aided the nursing home industry in exploiting him for profit. Public policies robbed him of any possibility of a productive and meaningful life. . . . In the end, David Rivlin chose the only option left him, and everyone clucked their tongues about how sad it all was" (42). Longmore speaks from experience—he too is disabled and on a ventilator, yet has persevered to live a full, meaningful life as a writer and professor—and as a euthanasia opponent.

Paragraph 6

For all of these reasons, disability rights activists have been the driving force in making physician-assisted suicide, a form of euthanasia, explicitly illegal in Iowa, Louisiana, Maryland, Michigan, Rhode Island, South Carolina, and Virginia. They have also worked tirelessly to defeat assisted suicide legislation in states like Alaska, California, Florida, Michigan, and Maine. They are among the loudest voices working to encourage America to be a society that encourages life over death and spend its energy seeking better care and pain management.

Paragraph 7

Make a list of all the transitions that appear in the essay and how they keep the ideas flowing.

The life of Larry McAfee offers a clear example of why the disabled must be allowed to live free of the various pressures brought on by the availability of euthanasia. Like Rivlin, McAfee relied on a ventilator to breathe after a spinal cord injury left him paralyzed. McAfee petitioned a Georgia court to have a doctor help end his life and was eventually granted it. Yet once given this "right to die," McAfee chose to live. He moved from a nursing home into an independent living facility he shared with other men who also had disabilities. In this place McAfee finally was able to live an interesting, happy life before dying naturally of a stroke eight years later. Surely, there was value in these additional eight years—value cherished by his friends, his family, and his community.

Paragraph 8

McAfee shows us the disabled are owed more than just the offer of a quick death. They deserve what all Americans deserve—the right to life, liberty, and the pursuit of happiness. Euthanasia robs the disabled of these rights. This is why nondisabled Americans must join the disabled community in fiercely opposing euthanasia and championing the rights of all Americans.

After reading the essay, are you convinced of the author's point? If so, what evidence swayed you? If not, why not?

Works Cited

Longmore, Paul K. "Policy, Prejudice, and Reality: Two Case Studies of Physician-Assisted Suicide." *Journal of Disability Policy Studies* (Summer 2005): 38–46.

Radtke, Richard. "A Case Against Physician-Assisted Suicide." *Journal of Disability Policy Studies* (Summer 2005): 58–61.

Exercise 3A: Examining Introductions and Conclusions

Every essay features introductory and concluding paragraphs that are used to frame the main ideas being presented. Along with presenting the essay's thesis statement, well-written introductions should grab the attention of the reader and make clear why the topic being explored is important. The conclusion reiterates the essay's thesis and is also the last chance for the writer to make an impression on the reader. Strong introductions and conclusions can greatly enhance an essay's effect on an audience.

The Introduction

There are several techniques that can be used to craft an introductory paragraph. An essay can start with:

- an anecdote: a brief story that illustrates a point relevant to the topic;
- startling information: facts or statistics that elucidate the point of the essay;
- setting up and knocking down a position: a position or claim believed by proponents of one side of a controversy, followed by statements that challenge that claim;
- historical perspective: an example of the way things used to be that leads into a discussion of how or why things work differently now;
- summary information: general introductory information about the topic that feeds into the essay's thesis statement.

1. Reread the introductory paragraphs of the model essays and of the viewpoints in Section One. Identify which of the techniques described above are used in the example essays. How do they grab the attention of the reader? Are their thesis statements clearly presented?
2. Write an introduction for the essay you have outlined and partially written in Exercise 1B using one of the techniques described above.

The Conclusion

The conclusion brings the essay to a close by summarizing or returning to its main ideas. Good conclusions, however, go beyond simply repeating these ideas. Strong conclusions explore a topic's broader implications and reiterate why it is important to consider. They may frame the essay by returning to an anecdote featured in the opening paragraph. Or they may close with a quotation or refer back to an event in the essay. In opinionated essays, the conclusion can reiterate which side the essay is taking or ask the reader to reconsider a previously held position on the subject.

3. Reread the concluding paragraphs of the model essays and of the viewpoints in Section One. Which were most effective in driving home their arguments to the reader? What sorts of techniques did they use to do this? Did they appeal emotionally to the reader or bookend an idea or event referenced elsewhere in the essay?

4. Write a conclusion for the essay you have outlined and partially written in Exercise 1B using one of the techniques described above.

Exercise 3B: Using Quotations to Enliven Your Essay

No essay is complete without quotations. Get in the habit of using quotes to support at least some of the ideas in your essays. Quotes do not need to appear in every paragraph, but often enough so that the essay contains voices aside from your own. When you write, use quotations to accomplish the following:

- Provide expert advice that you are not necessarily in the position to know about.
- Cite lively or passionate passages.
- Include a particularly well-written point that gets to the heart of the matter.
- Supply statistics or facts that have been derived from someone's research.

- Deliver anecdotes that illustrate the point you are trying to make.
- Express first-person testimony.

Problem One:

Reread the essays presented in all sections of this book and find at least one example of each of the above quotation types.

There are a couple of important things to remember when using quotations:

- Note your sources' qualifications and biases. This way your reader can identify the person you have quoted and can put their words in a context.
- Put any quoted material within proper quotation marks. Failing to attribute quotes to their authors constitutes plagiarism, which is when an author takes someone else's words or ideas and presents them as his or her own. Plagiarism is a very serious infraction and must be avoided at all costs.

Write Your Own Persuasive Five-Paragraph Essay

Using the information from this book, write your own five-paragraph persuasive essay that deals with euthanasia. You can use the resources in this book for information about issues relating to this topic and how to structure this type of essay.

The following steps are suggestions on how to get started.

Step One: Choose your topic.

The first step is to decide what topic to write your persuasive essay on. Is there anything that particularly fascinates you about euthanasia? Is there an aspect of the topic you strongly support, or feel strongly against? Is there an issue you feel personally connected to or one that you would like to learn more about? Ask yourself such questions before selecting your essay topic. Refer to Appendix D: Sample Essay Topics if you need help selecting a topic.

Step Two: Write down questions and answers about the topic.

Before you begin writing, you will need to think carefully about what ideas your essay will contain. This is a process known as *brainstorming*. Brainstorming involves asking yourself questions and coming up with ideas to discuss in your essay. Possible questions that will help you with the brainstorming process include:

- Why is this topic important?
- Why should people be interested in this topic?
- How can I make this essay interesting to the reader?
- What question am I going to address in this paragraph or essay?
- What facts, ideas, or quotes can I use to support the answer to my question?

Questions especially for persuasive essays include:
- Is there something I want to convince my reader of?
- Is there a topic I want to advocate in favor of or rally against?

- Is there enough evidence to support my opinion?
- Do I want to make a call to action—motivate my readers to do something about a particular problem or event?

Step Three: Gather facts, ideas, and anecdotes related to your topic.

This book contains several places to find information about many aspects of euthanasia, including the viewpoints and the appendices. In addition, you may want to research the books, articles, and Web sites listed in Section Three, or do additional research in your local library. You can also conduct interviews if you know someone who has a compelling story that would fit well in your essay.

Step Four: Develop a workable thesis statement.

Use what you have written down in steps two and three to help you articulate the main point or argument you want to make in your essay. It should be expressed in a clear sentence and make an arguable or supportable point.

Example:

Just like the government cannot tell us what to eat, when to sleep, or whom to love, it cannot judge for us when our own life has become too unbearable to be worth living.

This could be the thesis statement of a persuasive essay that argues that Americans have the right to die when and how they want.

Step Five: Write an outline or diagram.
1. Write the thesis statement at the top of the outline.
2. Write roman numerals I, II, and III on the left side of the page. Write letters A and B under each roman numeral.
3. Next to each roman numeral, write down the best ideas you came up with in step three. These should all directly relate to and support the thesis statement.
4. Next to each letter write down information that supports that particular idea.

Step Six: Write the three supporting paragraphs.
Use your outline to write the three supporting paragraphs. Write down the main idea of each paragraph in sentence form. Do the same thing for the supporting points of information. Each sentence should support the paragraph of the topic. Be sure you have relevant and interesting details, facts, and quotes. Use transitions when you move from idea to idea to keep the text fluid and smooth. Sometimes, although not always, paragraphs can include a concluding or summary sentence that restates the paragraph's argument.

Step Seven: Write the introduction and conclusion.
See Exercise 3A for information on writing introductions and conclusions.

Step Eight: Read and rewrite.
As you read, check your essay for the following:

- ✔ Does the essay maintain a consistent tone?
- ✔ Do all paragraphs reinforce your general thesis?
- ✔ Do all paragraphs flow from one to the other? Do you need to add transition words or phrases?
- ✔ Have you quoted from reliable, authoritative, and interesting sources?
- ✔ Is there a sense of progression throughout the essay?
- ✔ Does the essay get bogged down in too much detail or irrelevant material?
- ✔ Does your introduction grab the reader's attention?
- ✔ Does your conclusion reflect on any previously discussed material or give the essay a sense of closure?
- ✔ Are there any spelling or grammatical errors?

Section Three: Supporting Research Material

Facts About Euthanasia

Editor's Note: These facts can be used in reports to reinforce or add credibility when making important points or claims.

Euthanasia and the Law

Euthanasia is a doctor's ending a patient's life either by injection with lethal medication or by discontinuing life-saving treatment. It is often referred to as "mercy killing."

According to the news service Reuters and the BBC:
- A bill made euthanasia legal in Australia's Northern Territory in 1996, but it was overturned by the Australian Parliament in 1997.
- Euthanasia became legal in the Netherlands in 2001.
- Belgium legalized euthanasia in 2002.
- Euthanasia became legal in Luxembourg in 2008.

Physician-assisted suicide is a form of euthanasia in which a doctor prescribes a lethal medication to a patient, but the patient takes the medication on his or her own.

Assisted suicide is legal in:
- Switzerland (since 1941)
- Oregon (legal since 1994 and practiced since 1997)
- the Netherlands (since 2002)
- Washington (since 2008)
- Montana (since 2008, though as of 2009 a court decision to legalize it was being appealed)

Worldwide, physician-assisted suicide is explicitly illegal in Canada, Hungary, Italy, New Zealand, Norway, Russia, and the United Kingdom.

In the United States, physician-assisted suicide is explicitly illegal in Iowa, Louisiana, Maryland, Michigan, Rhode Island, South Carolina, and Virginia.

In 1997 the U.S. Supreme Court ruled in *Washington v. Glucksberg* and *Vacco v. Quill* that Americans do not have a constitutional right to die.

American Opinions About Euthanasia

A 2006 Gallup poll asked Americans whether they thought doctors should be allowed to end a terminally ill patient's life by some painless means if the patient and his or her family request it:

- 69 percent said yes.
- 27 percent said no.
- 4 percent were unsure.

A 2007 Associated Press–Ipsos poll found the following about American attitudes on euthanasia:

- 68 percent said sometimes there are circumstances in which a patient should be allowed to die.
- 30 percent said doctors and nurses should always do everything possible to save the life of a patient.
- 2 percent were unsure.
- 48 percent said it should be legal for doctors to help terminally ill patients end their own lives by giving them a prescription for lethal drugs.
- 44 percent said it should not be legal.
- 8 percent were unsure.
- 35 percent said if they were seriously ill with a terminal disease, they would consider ending their own life.
- 55 percent said they would not consider it.
- 5 percent said they might or would probably consider it.
- 5 percent were unsure.
- 53 percent of Americans think doctor Jack Kevorkian should not have been jailed for helping terminally ill people kill themselves.

- 40 percent believe he should have been jailed.
- 7 percent were unsure.

A 2005 poll by the Pew Research Center found the following about what Americans think about euthanasia:

- 74 percent of Americans said that if a patient with a terminal disease is unable to communicate and has not made his or her own wishes known in advance, the closest family member should be allowed to decide whether to continue medical treatment.
- 15 percent said the closest family member should not be allowed to decide.
- 5 percent said it depends.
- 70 percent of Americans said there are sometimes circumstances in which a patient should be allowed to die.
- 22 percent said doctors and nurses should always do everything possible to save a life.
- 8 percent were unsure.
- 84 percent of Americans approve of laws that let patients decide whether they want to be kept alive through medical treatment.
- 10 percent disapprove.
- 6 percent are unsure.
- 55 percent of Americans said it is sometimes justified to kill a spouse because he or she is suffering terrible pain from a terminal disease.
- 29 percent said this is never justified.
- 6 percent said this is always justified.
- 34 percent of Americans think the Democratic Party does a better job of dealing with issues related to end-of-life decisions.
- 22 percent of Americans think the Republican Party does a better job.
- 2 percent said they both deal equally with the issue.
- 16 percent think neither party deals well with the issue.
- 26 percent are unsure.

Finding and Using Sources of Information

No matter what type of essay you are writing, it is necessary to find information to support your point of view. You can use sources such as books, magazine articles, newspaper articles, and online articles.

Using Books and Articles

You can find books and articles in a library by using the library's computer or cataloging system. If you are not sure how to use these resources, ask a librarian to help you. You can also use a computer to find many magazine articles and other articles written specifically for the Internet.

You are likely to find a lot more information than you can possibly use in your essay, so your first task is to narrow it down to what is likely to be most usable. Look at book and article titles. Look at book chapter titles, and examine the book's index to see if it contains information on the specific topic you want to write about. (For example, if you want to write about euthanasia practices in the Netherlands and you find a book about assisted suicide, check the chapter titles and index to be sure it contains information about euthanasia and the Netherlands before you bother to check out the book.)

For a five-paragraph essay, you do not need a great deal of supporting information, so quickly try to narrow down your materials to a few good books and magazine or Internet articles. You do not need dozens. You might even find that one or two good books or articles contain all the information you need.

You probably do not have time to read an entire book, so find the chapters or sections that relate to your topic, and skim these. When you find useful information, copy it onto a note card or notebook. You should look for supporting facts, statistics, quotations, and examples.

Using the Internet

When you select your supporting information, it is important that you evaluate its source. This is especially important with information you find on the Internet. Because nearly anyone can put information on the Internet, there is as much bad information as good information. Before using Internet information—or any information—try to determine if the source seems to be reliable. Is the author or Internet site sponsored by a legitimate organization? Is it from a government source? Does the author have any special knowledge or training relating to the topic you are looking up? Does the article give any indication of where its information comes from?

Using Your Supporting Information

When you use supporting information from a book, article, interview, or other source, there are three important things to remember:

1. *Make it clear whether you are using a direct quotation or a paraphrase.* If you copy information directly from your source, you are quoting it. You must put quotation marks around the information and tell where the information comes from. If you put the information in your own words, you are paraphrasing it.

   Here is an example of a using a quotation:

   Many oppose euthanasia on the grounds that it is akin to "playing God." As one ethics professor put it, "Normalizing [euthanasia] would destroy a sense of the unfathomable mystery of life and seriously damage our human spirit, especially our capacity to find meaning in life" (Somerville).

Here is an example of a brief paraphrase of the same passage:

> Many oppose euthanasia on the grounds that it is akin to "playing God." Professor Margaret Somerville has expressed the commonly heard fear that making death routine, normal, and something controlled by humans will snuff out some of the very mystery that makes life worth living.

2. *Use the information fairly.* Be careful to use supporting information in the way the author intended it. For example, it is unfair to quote an author as saying "Euthanasia threatens the sacredness of life" when he or she intended to say, "Euthanasia threatens the sacredness of life as much as walking around a cancer ward puts a person at risk of catching cancer." This is called taking information out of context. This is using supporting evidence unfairly.

3. *Give credit where credit is due.* Giving credit is known as citing. You must use citations when you use someone else's information, but not every piece of supporting information needs a citation.

   - If the supporting information is general knowledge—that is, it can be found in many sources—you do not have to cite your source.
   - If you directly quote a source, you must cite it.
   - If you paraphrase information from a specific source, you must cite it. If you do not use citations where you should, you are *plagiarizing*—or stealing—someone else's work.

Citing Your Sources

There are a number of ways to cite your sources. Your teacher will probably want you to do it in one of three ways:

- Informal: As in the example in number 1 above, tell where you got the information as you present it in the text of your essay.

- Informal list: At the end of your essay, place an unnumbered list of all the sources you used. This tells the reader where, in general, your information came from.
- Formal: Use numbered footnotes or endnotes. Footnotes or endnotes are generally placed at the end of an article or essay, although they may be placed elsewhere depending on your teacher's requirements.

Works Cited

Somerville, Margaret. "The Case Against Euthanasia." *Ottawa Citizen* 27 Jun. 2008.

Using MLA Style to Create a Works Cited List

You will probably need to create a list of works cited for your paper. These include materials that you quoted from, relied heavily on, or consulted to write your paper. There are several different ways to structure these references. The following examples are based on Modern Language Association (MLA) style, one of the major citation styles used by writers.

Book Entries

For most book entries you will need the author's name, the book's title, where it was published, what company published it, and the year it was published. This information is usually found on the inside of the book. Variations on book entries include the following:

A book by a single author:
> Axworthy, Michael. *A History of Iran: Empire of the Mind.* New York: Basic Books, 2008.

Two or more books by the same author:
> Pollan, Michael. *In Defense of Food: An Eater's Manifesto.* New York: Penguin, 2009.
> ———. *The Omnivore's Dilemma.* New York: Penguin, 2006.

A book by two or more authors:
> Ronald, Pamela C., and R.W. Adamchak. *Tomorrow's Table: Organic Farming, Genetics, and the Future of Food.* New York: Oxford University Press, 2008.

A book with an editor:
> Friedman, Lauri S., ed. *Introducing Issues with Opposing Viewpoints: War*. Detroit: Greenhaven, 2009.

Periodical and Newspaper Entries

Entries for sources found in periodicals and newspapers are cited a bit differently from books. For one, these sources usually have a title and a publication name. They also may have specific dates and page numbers. Unlike book entries, you do not need to list where newspapers or periodicals are published or what company publishes them.

An article from a periodical:
> Hannum, William H., Gerald E. Marsh, and George S. Stanford. "Smarter Use of Nuclear Waste." *Scientific American* Dec. 2005: 84–91.

An unsigned article from a periodical:
> "Chinese Disease? The Rapid Spread of Syphilis in China." *Global Agenda* 14 Jan. 2007.

An article from a newspaper:
> Weiss, Rick. "Can Food from Cloned Animals Be Called Organic?" *Washington Post* 29 Jan. 2008: A06.

Internet Sources

To document a source you found online, try to provide as much information on it as possible, including the author's name, the title of the document, date of publication or of last revision, the URL, and your date of access.

A Web source:
> De Seno, Tommy. "*Roe Vs. Wade* and the Rights of the Father." Fox Forum.com (22 Jan. 2009) 20 May 2009 < http://foxforum.blogs.foxnews.com/2009/01/22/deseno_roe_wade/ > .

Your teacher will tell you exactly how information should be cited in your essay. Generally, the very least information needed is the original author's name and the name of the article or other publication.

Be sure you know exactly what information your teacher requires before you start looking for your supporting information so that you know what information to include with your notes.

Sample Essay Topics

Euthanasia Is Moral

Euthanasia Is Immoral

Euthanasia Devalues Life

Euthanasia Helps Cherish Life

Euthanasia Threatens the Old and Sick

Euthanasia Does Not Threaten the Old and Sick

Euthanasia Threatens the Disabled

Euthanasia Does Not Threaten the Disabled

Euthanasia Threatens Undesirable Groups of People

Euthanasia Poses No Threat to Any Group of People

Euthanasia Respects a Person's Right to Die

There Is No Such Thing As the Right to Die

Legalized Euthanasia Has Hurt People in Other Countries

Legalized Euthanasia Has Helped People in Other Countries

Good End-of-Life Care Can Make Euthanasia Unnecessary

Good End-of-Life Care Includes the Option of Euthanasia

Children Should Sometimes Receive Euthanasia

Children Should Never Receive Euthanasia

People in a Persistent Vegetative State Should Receive Euthanasia

People in a Persistent Vegetative State Should Not Receive Euthanasia

The Terminally Ill Should Receive Euthanasia

The Terminally Ill Should Not Receive Euthanasia

The Severely Handicapped Should Sometimes Receive Euthanasia

Organizations to Contact

The editor has compiled the following list of organizations concerned with the issues debated in this book. The descriptions are derived from materials provided by the organizations. All have publications or information available for interested readers. The list was compiled on the date of publication of the present volume; the information provided here may change. Be aware that many organizations take several weeks or longer to respond to queries, so allow as much time as possible.

American Civil Liberties Union (ACLU)
125 Broad St., 18th Flr., New York, NY 10004
Web site: www.aclu.org

The ACLU champions the rights of individuals in right-to-die and euthanasia cases as well as in many other civil rights issues. The Foundation of the ACLU provides legal defense, research, and education. The organization publishes the quarterly *Civil Liberties* and various pamphlets, books, and position papers.

The American Life League (ALL)
PO Box 1350, Stafford, VA 22555 • (540) 659-4171
e-mail: info@all.org • Web site: www.all.org

ALL believes that human life is sacred. As such, it opposes euthanasia and assisted suicide and works to educate Americans on its position. It publishes the bimonthly pro-life magazine *Celebrate Life*.

American Society of Law, Medicine, and Ethics
765 Commonwealth Ave., Ste. 1634, Boston, MA 02215
(617) 262-4990 • e-mail: info@aslme.org
Web site: www.aslme.org

The American Society of Law, Medicine, and Ethics has an information clearinghouse and a library, and it acts as a forum for discussion of issues such as euthanasia and assisted suicide. The society's members include physicians, attorneys, health-care administrators, and others interested in the relationship between law, medicine, and ethics.

Autonomy, Inc.

14 Strawberry Hill Ln., Danvers, MA 01923 • (617) 320-0506
e-mail: info@autonomynow.org • Web site: www.autonomy now.org

Autonomy, Inc. represents the interests of disabled people who want legal, safe access to physician-assisted suicide. The organization also supports Oregon's Death with Dignity Act and has filed important papers in major right-to-die cases. Its Web site offers articles and an extensive bibliography of readings about how euthanasia affects the disabled.

Dignity in Dying

181 Oxford St., London W1D 2JT • 44 + 020 7479 7730
e-mail: info@dignityindying.org.uk • Web site: www.dignity indying.org.uk

Formerly the Voluntary Euthanasia Society, this British group seeks to legalize physician-assisted suicide in the United Kingdom. Its mission is to secure the right for people to be able to die with dignity at the end of their lives. In addition to information on the issue, its Web site offers compelling stories and first-person testimonials.

Dying with Dignity

55 Eglinton Ave. East, Ste. 802, Toronto, ON M4P 1G8, Canada • (800) 495-6156 • e-mail: info@dyingwith dignity.ca • Web site: www.dyingwithdignity.ca

Dying with Dignity seeks to make physician-assisted suicide legal in Canada. It participates in educational and counseling efforts for individuals faced with making important end-of-life decisions. The group also seeks to improve hospice and palliative care services.

Euthanasia Prevention Coalition

Box 25033, London, ON N6C 6A8 Canada • (877) 439-3348 e-mail: info@epcc.ca • Web site: www.epcc.ca

Based in Ontario, Canada, this group educates and informs organizations and individuals to help them create social barriers against euthanasia and physician-assisted suicide. The group offers information packages for schools, churches, politicians, hospice and palliative care groups, and the general public.

Euthanasia Research and Guidance Organization (ERGO)

24829 Norris Ln., Junction City, OR 97448-9559
(541) 998-1873 • e-mail: ergo@efn.org • Web site: www .finalexit.org

ERGO is a nonprofit organization founded to educate patients, physicians, and the general public about euthanasia and physician-assisted suicide. The organization serves a broad range of people: It provides research for students, other "right-to-die" organizations, authors, and journalists; conducts opinion polls; drafts guidelines about how to prepare for and commit assisted suicide for physicians and patients; and counsels dying patients as long as they are competent adults in the final stages of a terminal illness.

Human Life International (HLI)

4 Family Life Ln., Front Royal, VA 22630 • (800) 549-5433 fax: (540) 622-6247 • e-mail: hli@hli.org • Web site: www .hli.org

HLI is opposed to euthanasia and believes assisted suicide is morally unacceptable. It defends the rights of the unborn, the disabled, and those threatened by euthanasia, and provides education, advocacy, and support services on the matter.

International Anti-Euthanasia Task Force (IAETF)
PO Box 760, Steubenville, OH 43952 • (740) 282-3810
e-mail: info@iaetf.org • Web site: www.iaetf.org

The IAETF works to prevent assisted suicide from becoming legal in both the United States and abroad. Its Web site and publications address the issues of euthanasia, assisted suicide, advance directives, assisted suicide proposals, right-to-die assisted suicide in Oregon, legal cases, euthanasia practices in the Netherlands, disability rights, and pain control.

National Hospice and Palliative Care Organization
1700 Diagonal Rd., Ste. 625, Alexandria, Virginia 22314
(703) 837-1500 • e-mail: nhpco_info@nhpco.org
Web site: www.nho.org

The National Hospice and Palliative Care Organization supports the idea that with the proper care and pain medication, the terminally ill can live out their lives comfortably and in the company of their families. As such, it opposes assisted suicide and works to educate the public about the benefits of hospice care for the terminally ill and their families.

National Right to Life Committee (NRLC)
512 Tenth St. NW, Washington, DC 20004
(202) 626-8800 • e-mail: NRLC@nrlc.org
Web site: www.nrlc.org

The NRLC opposes euthanasia and assisted suicide. It publishes the monthly *NRL News* and many articles from an anti-euthanasia perspective.

The Right to Die Society of Canada
145 Macdonell Ave., Toronto, ON M6R 2A4 Canada
(416) 535-0690 • e-mail: contact-rtd@righttodie.ca
Web site: www.righttodie.ca

This Canadian organization supports the right of any mature individual who is chronically or terminally ill to choose the time, place, and means of his or her death. Its publications include *Free to Go*, a publication that features pro-assisted suicide and euthanasia articles.

Bibliography

Books

Dowbiggin, Ian, *A Concise History of Euthanasia: Life, Death, God, and Medicine*. Lanham, MD: Rowman & Littlefield, 2007.

Gorsuch, Neil M., *The Future of Assisted Suicide and Euthanasia*. Princeton, NJ: Princeton University Press, 2009.

Lively, Brian, *The Dying Keats: A Case for Euthanasia?* Leicester, UK: Matador, 2009.

Nicol, Neal, and Harry Wylie, *Between the Dying and the Dead: Dr. Jack Kevorkian's Life and the Battle to Legalize Euthanasia*. Madison: University of Wisconsin Press, 2006.

Pappas, Demetra M., *Euthanasia/Assisted Suicide Debate*. Santa Barbara, CA: ABC-CLIO/Greenwood, 2009.

Smith, Wesley J., *Forced Exit: Euthanasia, Assisted Suicide and the New Duty of Die*. New York: Encounter, 2006.

Periodicals

Ayliffe, Nahum, "Euthanasia—Dying with Dignity?" *National Forum* (Australia), February 7, 2007.

Bellieni, Carlo, "'Quality of Life' Is a Misnomer: The Case for Neonatal Euthanasia," *Journal of Medicine and the Person*, vol. 4, no. 3, September 2006.

Crumley, Bruce, "Making a Case for Euthanasia," *Time*, March 15, 2008.

Cunningham, Roseanna, "Care, Not Euthanasia, Is the Answer to the 'Problem' of the Elderly," *Times* (London), July 20, 2008.

Deane, Alex, "The Case Against Euthanasia," Conservative Home.com, platform, May 16, 2006.

Ferrari, Marie Jeanne, "Is There an Alternative to Euthanasia?" *Catholic Insight*, vol. 16, no. 10, November 2008.

Greenblatt, Jerome, "The Case for Euthanasia," *Let Life In*, April 2, 2008.

Hardt, John J., "Church Teaching and My Father's Choice; 'Medically Ordinary' Does Not Always Mean Morally Ordinary," *America*, January 21, 2008.

Heide, Agnes van der, et al., "End-of-Life Practices in the Netherlands Under the Euthanasia Act," *New England Journal of Medicine*, May 10, 2007.

Knox, Noelle, "An Agonizing Debate About Euthanasia," *USA Today*, November 22, 2005.

Moffic, H. Steven, "Dr. Death and the Meaning of Life," *Clinical Psychiatry News*, September 2007.

Mohler, Albert, "Euthanasia for Newborns—Killing in the Netherlands," AlbertMohler.com, March 14, 2005.

Palmer, Alasdair, "Why We Must Not Make the 'Right to Die' Legal," *Telegraph* (London), June 8, 2008.

Rigali, Justin, and Bishop William Lori, "In Defense of Human Dignity: On Providing Food and Fluids to Helpless Patients," *America*, October 13, 2008.

Rosner, Fred, "Euthanasia: Biblical and Rabbinic Sources," MyJewishLearning.com, 2009.

Seligman, Katherine, "Hastening the End," *San Francisco Chronicle*, June 8, 2008.

Smith, Wesley J., "Euthanasia Comes to Montana," *Weekly Standard*, vol. 14, no. 15, December 29, 2008.

Sokol, Ronald, "Essay: The Right to Die," *New York Times*, March 21, 2007.

Somerville, Margaret, "The Case Against Euthanasia," *Ottawa* (ON) *Citizen*, June 27, 2008.

Web Sites

Compassion & Choices (www.compassionandchoices .org). This is the oldest and largest pro-euthanasia organization in the United States. Its Web site discusses pain management, improving end-of-life care, and efforts to legalize assisted suicide.

The Death with Dignity National Center (www.dwd.org). This group's mission is to expand end-of-life choices and advance the legalization of physician aid in dying. Its Web site offers a plethora of articles, editorials, and news updates from a pro-euthanasia perspective.

Euthanasia.com (www.euthanasia.com). Offers an exhaustive archive of research materials about euthanasia, mostly from an anti-euthanasia perspective.

Euthanasia and Physician Assisted Suicide (www.religious tolerance.org/euthanas.htm). A thorough site with varying perspectives on the right to die, public opinion polls, and religious beliefs about hastened dying.

International Task Force on Euthanasia and Assisted Suicide (www.internationaltaskforce.org). Founded to combat efforts to legalize euthanasia and physician-assisted suicide, this organization's main site offers links to news updates about efforts to legalize assisted suicide, as well as various articles about euthanasia and pain management.

The Nightingale Alliance (www.nightingalealliance.org). The Nightingale Alliance opposes the legalization of euthanasia and physician-assisted suicide. This Web site offers brochures and numerous links to news articles, pain management information, personal stories, research papers, arguments against euthanasia, and more.

Not Dead Yet (www.notdeadyet.org). This group represents disabled people who oppose euthanasia. Its Web site offers many archived articles, fact sheets, and links from an anti-euthanasia perspective.

The World Federation of Right to Die Societies (www.worldrtd.net). This group consists of thirty-eight organizations in twenty-three countries all fighting to legalize euthanasia and physician-assisted suicide. Its Web site offers plentiful resources, newsletters, and articles on the subject.

Index

S
Sauer, Pieter, 27
Schiavo, Terri, 16
Sebire, Chantal, 9, 30
Singer, Peter, 26–33
Slippery slope argument, 14, 53–54
Somerville, Margaret, 50–51, 53, 55–56
St. Peter's University Hospital, 31
State paternalism, 9
Switzerland, 23, 37

U
United Nations Human Rights Commission, 7

United States, 23, 31–33
Universal Declaration of Human Rights (UNDHR), 7

V
Vacco v. Quill (1997), 7, 37
Verhagen, Eduaard, 27
Voluntary euthanasia, 16

W
Washington v. Glucksberg (1997), 7, 37

Y
Youk, Thomas, 16, 37

Picture Credits

About the Editor

Lauri S. Friedman earned her bachelor's degree in religion and political science from Vassar College in Poughkeepsie, New York. Her studies there focused on political Islam. Friedman has worked as a non-fiction writer, a newspaper journalist, and an editor for more than eight years. She has extensive experience in both academic and professional settings.

Friedman is the founder of LSF Editorial, a writing and editing business in San Diego. She has edited and authored numerous publications for Greenhaven Press on controversial social issues such as oil, the Internet, the Middle East, democracy, pandemics, and obesity. Every book in the *Writing the Critical Essay* series has been under her direction or editorship, and she has personally written more than eighteen titles in the series. She was instrumental in the creation of the series, and played a critical role in its conception and development.